Charts on
Systematic Theology

Volume 1
Prolegomena

KREGEL
CHARTS OF THE BIBLE
AND THEOLOGY

Charts on Systematic Theology

Volume 1
Prolegomena

H. Wayne House

with Kyle Roberts

Kregel
Academic & Professional

Charts on Systematic Theology, Volume 1: Prolegomena

© 2006 by H. Wayne House

Published by Kregel Publications, a division of Kregel, Inc., P.O. Box 2607, Grand Rapids, MI 49501.

ISBN 0-8254-2771-1

Printed in the United States of America

06 07 08 09 10 / 5 4 3 2 1

To
my students at
Faith Evangelical Seminary,
Tacoma, Washington,
and Salem, Oregon.

Contents

Preface

Systematic theology has been known in the past as the queen of the sciences, the term "science" referring to fields of knowledge (from the Latin word *scientia*, meaning "knowledge"). The science of the study of God is indeed worthy of our best efforts and most serious attention. Systematic theology builds on its primary source, the biblical text, but is informed by other areas of knowledge including history, science, logic, and philosophy. Consequently, there are many issues that should be studied prior to the formal study of systematic theology. These matters include the nature of theology, the possibility of doing systematic theology, the various categories of theology, approaches to doctrine, the nature of divine revelation, the possibility and manner of knowing God and speaking about God, the science of biblical and theological interpretation, the function and distinction of faith and reason, the source and nature of truth, and how the two Testaments of the Bible relate to one another.

Each of the above areas is included within this first volume of *Charts on Systematic Theology*. The organized chart format facilitates easy comparison and digestion of different perspectives, and readers will discover by the use of these charts the considerable diversity of thought among theologians. This volume is intended to be a supplement for the interested student of theology. Although some contemporary theologies have chosen not to include in any detail the introductory subjects underpinning theology and its interpretation, this work is offered as an introduction to those important preliminary considerations.

H. Wayne House
Distinguished Research Professor of Biblical and Theological Studies
Faith Evangelical Seminary

Acknowledgments

Anytime one writes a book there are many people who should be thanked for their contributions to the book. The completion of this book is likewise due to the efforts of many.

The first person I wish to thank is my researcher, Dr. Kyle Roberts. When we started this project he was a doctoral student at Trinity Evangelical Divinity School. He now holds a position in the theology department of Bethel Seminary. His work was invaluable to the production of this work of theology.

Dr. Michael Adams, dean of Faith Evangelical Seminary, has continued his graciousness toward me in allowing considerable time as a research professor to pursue various writing projects such as this. Dennis Jowers, assistant professor of apologetics and theology at Faith Evangelical Seminary, read an early draft of the book. Additionally, my students at Faith Evangelical Seminary have enabled me to fine-tune the work during class instruction for the benefit of others.

Dennis Hillman, publisher at Kregel Publications, has been faithful to our "grand plan" in producing a number of integrative works on theology that we scratched out on a paper tablecloth in Colorado Springs years ago. We have worked together on a number of projects, and he always proves to be supportive of my efforts. The editor of the book, Paul Ingram, needs to be mentioned. His attention to detail has enabled me to offer to the public an accurate and readable work.

Last of all, I thank my wife, Leta, for her moral support to my labors throughout more than thirty-eight years of marriage.

PART ONE
What Is Theology?

Introductory Issues

There are many ways to define theology. The approaches to and purposes of theology span a spectrum that cannot be fully represented in these pages. There are as many definitions (or conceptions) of theology as there are theologians. It is possible, however, to locate common elements of definition, recognizing that individual theologians will overlap and share commonalities with those represented by other types. To say a theologian or a particular type of theology is "A" does not mean that the theologian shares or exhibits none of the elements of "B," or of "C."

We ask the question "What is theology?" in a normative sense. That is, what should theology be and do? This section is not interested in what theology *happens to be* at the moment as a practiced discipline. This is not a "state of the theological union" discussion so much as an inquiry into what theologians (past and present) view their task to be.

A LINE IN THE SAND?

At the height of the Enlightenment, Immanuel Kant (1724–1804) divided knowledge into two kinds (practical and pure). This distinction was connected to his theory of the difference between *phenomena* and *noumena*. *Phenomena* are the appearances of things as we see, touch, and empirically observe the world around us. The *noumena* are the things-in-themselves, the objects of our perceptions. We only have knowledge of things insofar as we have perceptions of them and only as the things-in-themselves appear to us. The innate structure of our mind provides the possibility of a kind of scientific certainty of everyday, observable things.

The objects of religion (God, the supernatural, etc.), however, are not elements of *pure knowledge*, because they are not observable in this way. Thus for Kant *practical knowledge*, not *pure knowledge*, is the only genuine object of theology. Our acquisition of practical knowledge is severely limited, and metaphysics reduced to a discussion of practical knowledge is an impossible discipline. God becomes only a necessary postulate of ethics. We *need* God's existence in order for society to be ethical, so a God must exist. Also, if there was no God, there would be no eternal reward for our actions on earth. We have a desire and a need to live well and to respect others (the "categorial imperative"), so God's existence is necessary and belief in God is justified—though not the God of traditional Christian doctrine and Scripture (revelation).[1] Kant located the heart of religion in ethics, doing theology very much "from below." Since we cannot gain reliable knowledge of God through revelation, we must learn to know Him by observing human actions here on earth.

Theologies after Kant have taken one of two roads. We are taught either that we can have certain knowledge of God and the supernatural through the means He has provided (various modes of revelation), or they affirm, with Kant, the need to ground theology in human reason (and perception) alone.

This brings us to our primary definitions of theology. We have chosen the two broad categories of "subjective" and "objective." Within these categories, we will locate more specific examples of thinking about the broader subject. We will go beyond merely dividing theologians or theologies by ideology, to discovering relationships from ideas, and to the overall goals, aims, and possibilities for theology. It would perhaps be better to think of these categories as "primarily objective" and "primarily subjective," because there are elements of both in all theologies.

"OBJECTIVE THEOLOGIES"

Objective theologies recognize and pay conscious heed to the "objective" dimension of theology, or the "realism principle."[2] Those in this philosophical position affirm that the world as we see it, experience it, and

What Is Theology?

come to know it is truly and basically (though not perfectly or completely) what it *appears to be*. We can come to know and understand the natural and the supernatural with some degree of certainty. These theologies will generally prioritize God's revelation in the *knowing* process. It also may be possible for an "objective theology" to prioritize human reason so long as human reason is affirmed as a genuine way to come to know God (e.g., natural theology) and His relations with the world. Objective theologies focus on the transcendent nature of truth. God has made Himself known through the world He created and through His Word. His revelation is unchanging, although experiences and interpretations of it vary. For objective theologies, human knowledge is not utterly relegated by historical situation, or cultural and linguistic expression, to perspectival knowledge. Objective theologies affirm, to one degree or another, that it is possible to acquire and understand transcendent truth (e.g., God and His relationship to the world) with some confidence and adequacy. The task for objective theologies is to articulate the reality of the transcendent God and His relation to the created order in new situations and contexts. Objective theologies, in the main, seek to do theology "from above." That is, they desire to know, insofar as it may be possible, either what God Himself knows (to a limited degree) or what God has provided for people to know about Him.

"SUBJECTIVE THEOLOGIES"

Subjective theologies, in the main, follow Kant's reasoning and side with skepticism regarding knowledge of God and of supernatural reality apart from our constructive apprehensions of it. Those following the subjective path pay attention to the "bias principle," which focuses on the perspectival nature of knowledge and truth.[3]

They seek to answer many of the same kinds of questions as those of objective theologies (who — or what — is God, what is humanity, what is sin, etc.), but they do so by turning to the realm of human experience, religious feeling, the affective power of symbolism and of metaphorical expression, etc. Subjective theologians focus on the historical situatedness of knowledge (and thus of theology). Since knowledge is historically, culturally, and linguistically conditioned, all *theology* is a personal perspective, an individuated (though not necessarily *individual*) response to the reality of *God* and of divine things. Subjective theologians will have a greater or lesser respect for whether there might be a "God's-eye-view" of things, but all will be keenly sensitive to our limitations in knowing it. They will sometimes be more interested in what theology can do for their respective communities of influence (e.g., as in liberation theology) than in whether theology is adequately grasping reality "out there" (as in metaphysical theologies). They will also have a greater or lesser respect for the traditions of theology. For some, Christian theological traditions provide an invaluable and indispensable resource to the work of theology. For others, tradition (councils, creeds, etc.) is simply a hindrance to thinking (and theologizing) clearly and effectively for oneself. Subjective theologies will often approach theology through history or philosophy. Theology then becomes simply religious studies, a history of religious experience or a philosophy of religion, in a merely descriptive sense. Subjective theologies are theologies "from below." That is, they recognize that there is only one possible way to acquire any knowledge at all of God — through the observation and experience of being human in the world God has created.

---

1. Alan G. Padgett, "Immanuel Kant," in *The Dictionary of Historical Theology,* ed. Trevor Hart (Grand Rapids: Eerdmans, 2000), 296–97.
2. Richard Lints defines the "realism principle" this way: "Individuals normally know the world pretty much as it is." *The Fabric of Theology* (Grand Rapids: Eerdmans, 1993), 20.
3. Here is Lints's definition of the "bias principle": "Individuals never know the world apart from biases that influence their view of what really is the case." Ibid.

Objective Theologies			Theology as Conversation and Proclamation
Theology as Science (Rationality)	Theology as Search for Understanding/Wisdom	Theology as Ministry	
Charles Hodge, Thomas F. Torrance, B. B. Warfield	Augustine, Daniel Migliore, Thomas Aquinas	John Calvin, John Frame	Richard Lints, Helmut Thielicke

Theology as Science (Rationality)

Theology is a science like other sciences, having a proper, communally agreed-upon method of research gathering, hypotheses testing, and assessment/analysis that leads toward a conclusion. In such a scientific approach, it would be assumed that the same conclusions would be reached by anyone approaching the same task using the same methods. Thus, in answer to the question "Who is God?" the theologian would simply gather the requisite data from Scripture and/or from general revelation, depending on the theologian's emphasis, and analyze the data to formulate a conclusion about the nature and being of God: (e.g., God is a Trinity who is omnipotent, omniscient, and who interacts with the world in such and such a way). For B. B. Warfield, one example of this view, theology is "that science which treats of God and of the relations between God and the universe."[4] Theology, for Warfield, seeks after the "ideally true"; thus it "deals with absolute truth and aims at organizing into a concatenated system all the truth in its sphere."[5] The "truth," for Warfield, is found in "facts" of the subject, which, in the main, are found in Scripture.[6]

Warfield distinguishes between the study of theology and the study of religion as belonging to two "spheres," though sharing the same base of "facts." Theology has as its subject matter the knowledge of God and His

Theology as Search for Understanding/Wisdom

Theology is "a continuing search for the fullness of the truth of God made known in Jesus Christ."[15] This definition, which begins Migliore's basic theology text, *Faith Seeking Understanding*, captures the essence of the view of theology as a "search." It is a search for understanding (wisdom), for truth and the appropriation of truth to one's life, a search for meaning, and, ultimately, a search for God Himself. Migliore suggests, "Theology is not mere repetition of traditional doctrines but a persistent search for the truth to which they point and which they only partially and brokenly express."[16] Theology is a "continuing inquiry," and thus its ethos is "interrogative" or even dialogical, rather than "doctrinaire."[17]

This view approaches the task of theology in a personal or subjective light. Its method is more organic than mechanistic. There may be multiple appropriate methods, processes, approaches, and systems for doing theology. So long as a genuine search for the truth of God is taking place, the work of theology is being done.

These are "objective theologies" because a search presupposes a desired object that lies outside the one searching. In the case of theology, when the object is either a gift of God (e.g., salvation, knowledge, etc.) or God Himself (relational knowledge of God), the *real* existence of the object takes precedence over

Theology as Ministry

John Calvin (1509–64) wrote his *Institutes of the Christian Religion* to help "those who desire to be instructed in the doctrine of salvation" and to serve as a "key to open a way for all children of God into a good and right understanding of Holy Scripture."[21] Calvin connected an adequate understanding of Scripture and of the doctrine of salvation with growth in the Christian life. Indeed, for Calvin, the knowledge of God and the knowledge of ourselves are intricately related. We do not have one without the other. The theologian is a minister and theology is a ministry. As he stated, "The theologian's task is not to divert the ears with chatter, but to strengthen consciences by teaching things true, sure, and profitable."[22]

In our own day, John Frame divides aspects of theology into three: normative, situational, and existential. The existential aspect is the realm of human life—what does this mean for me here and now? Theology is, for Frame, a "secondary description"; it is a "reinterpretation" of all of the diverse content of Scripture. He says that we need this reinterpretation "to *meet human needs*": "The job of theology is to help people understand the Bible better, not to give an abstractly perfect account of the truth, regardless of whether anyone understands it. The job of theology is to teach people the truth of God"[23] He defines theology as "the application of the Word of

Theology as Conversation and Proclamation

Focusing on the dialogical, or relational, aspect of theology, theology is a conversation or an encounter with the living God in Word and Spirit. It is also a communication of truth and ideas—from the theologian to his or her community.

Helmut Thielicke draws an important distinction between *ontic* (metaphysical or physical reality) and *noetic* (the knowledge of that reality) elements of theology. *Ontic* both precedes and supercedes the *noetic*. We have knowledge (*noetic*) of God only because we exist in a real (*ontic*) relationship with God.

The subject of theology for Thielicke is the correlation between lost humans and God. As he says, "the consciousness of this correlation is not itself the subject; the subject is the real, living active God in relationship with his creation." This relationship is understood through the consciousness. That understanding presupposes a reality behind what is understood. It is, Thielicke says, an "'echo' of that which ontically defines man's existence."[29]

Thielicke defines the task of theology thusly: "To do theology is to actualize Christian truth, or, better, to set it forth in its actuality and to understand it afresh thereby."[30]

Theology is always a historical discipline; that is, we (the theologian) are trapped in a historical situation. In response to this

What Is Theology?

	Objective Theologies		Theology as Conversation and Proclamation
Theology as Science (Rationality)	**Theology as Search for Understanding/Wisdom**	**Theology as Ministry**	
Hodge, Torrance, Warfield	Augustine, Migliore, Aquinas	Calvin, Frame	Lints, Thielicke

Theology as Science (Rationality) — Hodge, Torrance, Warfield

relation to His creatures; therefore it is "objective." Religion has as its subject matter the study of humanity (its "aspirations and imaginings"), therefore it is "subjective."[7] Because theology is a science, he asserts, there can be "but one theology."[8]

The benefits of this view include the high seriousness with which it views the task of theology and the place of importance that Scripture is accorded. It boasts of an innate optimism about discovering absolute truth and about the ability of facts to lead to the true view of things, if only the correct procedure is followed.

By way of criticism, the view betrays some naiveté regarding the historical situatedness of knowledge and the interpreted nature of facts. "Brute facts" do not exist. They always come *with* interpretations, either of the presenter or the audience. What exactly are "facts" for the theologian? Metaphors? Doctrines? Are metaphors doctrines? Are doctrines metaphorical? Does the Old Testament contain "facts" in the same way as the New Testament? Which facts are allowed priority in a theological system? And further, history has shown that there simply is not "one theology."—Warfield's ideal. There are as many theologies, from the human perspective anyway, as there are theologians. Is this only a result of not following the correct "scientific" method?

Other prominent theologians who operate

Theology as Search for Understanding/Wisdom — Augustine, Migliore, Aquinas

the knowledge (and perception) of the one who is seeking. Thus, theology is an act of worship from the beginning. The knowing subject (the theologian) humbles him/herself before the object being sought and known. The more that is known and understood about God, the more satisfied are the yearnings of the searcher. And yet, more and different "thirsts" may arise in consequence.

This view takes seriously Paul's reminder that we see through a glass darkly and that we can have knowledge, in this life, only in part (1 Cor. 13). However, this does not undermine the significance of seeking a conceptual, objective knowledge of God. Rather, theology, since it seeks after the knowledge of God, is the highest search one could undertake.

Many theologians could be said to subscribe to this view. Certainly all genuine Christians seek after the knowledge of God and seek after wisdom. But in some theologies the concept of seeking and the emphasis on limitations of conceptual knowledge are prominent. Augustine (our hearts are restless until they find rest in God) and Anselm (faith seeking understanding) are well-known exemplars of this perspective.

Kevin Vanhoozer[18] in *The Drama of Doctrine* suggests that the task of theology is not a merely conceptual enterprise in which the theologian compiles a list of propositions. Rather, it is a way of *wisdom*, the "stuff of

Theology as Ministry — Calvin, Frame

God by persons to all areas of life." Application means, Frame notes, simply "teaching" or "doctrine" of the Scriptures. "Teaching in the New Testament (and I think also in the Old) is the use of God's revelation to meet the spiritual needs of people, to promote godliness and spiritual health."[24]

What Christian theologian would not think of theology as having (or desiring to have), at least as an indirect result, a positive effect on the people of God? But for Calvin and for Frame, the primary aim of theology seems to be twofold: (1) the understanding of the Scriptures and (2) the salvation, sanctification and spiritual health of those who so understand them. Whereas someone could imagine a nonbeliever doing theology as a "science," it would be difficult to imagine him/her doing theology as a ministry!

This view has much in common with the *theology as search* perspective. The difference might simply lie in its ethos and assumptions. A proponent of the *theology as ministry* model could work under the false impression or suggestion that the theologian's task is to understand the truth (doctrines, theological formulations) and then to apply those truths to life as if they are separate in nature. Further, one could be under the mistaken assumption that, having learned everything there is to know about Scripture, he or she is complete in sanctification. *Theology as search* implies that the theologian is a fellow sojourner on

Theology as Conversation and Proclamation — Lints, Thielicke

"problem," however, the word of proclamation (the biblical message) comes to us in an encounter. It is an "encounter that concerns man's existence, that touches his personal core, his heart, so that it applies to him unconditionally."[31] Because of the encounter/relational aspect of Christian truth, analogies (ways of understanding God through human language) can truly capture the reality of God and His relations with the world. Theology then, simply seeks to "address," or "readdress," Christian truth to each new historical situation. Thielicke distinguishes his theology of "address," or "actualizing," from that of "accommodation, in which the truth is subservient to the individual" (the truth is "under me") and his/her historical situation.

According to Richard Lints, "Theology must first be about a conversation with God," which began at creation and continued with the fall. He suggests that, "The Christian theological framework is all about understanding the speech of God and appropriating it in the lives of those he has called out. Thus, the theological framework is primarily about listening—listening to God himself."[32]

This view has the benefit of giving Scripture practical authority in the theological task to ask the theologian questions about his or her own life—and whether or not Christian truth has been appropriated, or actualized, in his or her being. Thus theology is seen not as simply a discipline for acquiring

What Is Theology?

Objective Theologies

Theology as Science (Rationality)	Theology as Search for Understanding/Wisdom	Theology as Ministry	Theology as Conversation and Proclamation
Hodge, Torrance, Warfield	Augustine, Migliore, Aquinas	Calvin, Frame	Lints, Thielicke

Theology as Science (Rationality) — Hodge, Torrance, Warfield

under a similar model as Warfield are Charles Hodge, Gerhaardus Vos, and more currently, Wayne Grudem and Gordon Clark. A theologian whose sensibilities differ from those of Warfield but who also defines theology as a science is Thomas F. Torrance. An accomplished scientist as well as a theologian, Torrance defines theology as "the positive science in which we think only in accordance with the nature of the given."[9] For Torrance, "Theology and every scientific inquiry operate with the correlation of the intelligible and the intelligent."[10] Torrance views theology as a "metascience of our direct cognitive relation to God."[11] We need to do theology because our limited, finite perspective demands a rigorously cognitive probing "in obedience to the demands of His reality and self-giving."[12] Ultimately, it is God's reality that we seek to know and understand, but we must do this through utilizing our own scientific, rational capacities. For Torrance, humanity is the "enemy" in this task, but the necessary subject who seeks after the knowledge of the object, God's reality.

Alister McGrath, an evangelical historical theologian, has proposed the interaction between theology and science as a fertile ground for exploring the benefits that each discipline might gain from a mutual interchange.[13] His project "aims to examine, critically yet appreciatively, the way in which the working assumptions and methods of Christian theology

Theology as Search for Understanding/Wisdom — Augustine, Migliore, Aquinas

life." This view, Vanhoozer notes, overcomes the "theory/practice dichotomy." Because the subject matter of theology is "Jesus Christ . . . the way, the truth and the life," theology "must deal with truth, with ways of living, and with the meaning of life."[19] Theological competence, Vanhoozer says, is "ultimately a matter of being able to make judgments that display the mind of Christ." Likening the task of theology in the church to that of a drama, Vanhoozer suggests, "the drama of doctrine is about refining the dross of textual knowledge into the gold of Christian wisdom by putting one's understanding of the Scriptures into practice . . . the proper end of the drama of doctrine is wisdom: lived knowledge, a performance of the truth."[20]

15. Daniel Migliore, *Faith Seeking Understanding* (Grand Rapids: Eerdmans, 1991), 1.
16. Ibid.
17. Ibid.
18. Kevin J. Vanhoozer, *The Drama of Doctrine: A Canonical-linguistic Approach to Christian Theology* (Louisville: Westminster/John Knox, 2005).
19. Ibid.
20. Ibid.

Theology as Ministry — Calvin, Frame

the way, not simply a guide or teacher of travelers.

Ellen Charry attempts to wed the conceptual knowledge of God with its application to spiritual formation. In her book *By the Renewing of Your Minds: The Pastoral Function of Christian Doctrine*,[25] Charry presents a fresh look at several significant historical theologians who saw the task of theology as directly impacting the personal, spiritual lives of themselves and their readers. She has presented these theologians anew "so that we might be stirred up to take up the task they were engaged in: helping people flourish through knowing and loving God."[26]

Charry could just as legitimately be placed under the *theology as wisdom* category, for she emphasizes the "sapiential" nature of theological truth: "The norm of sapience [wisdom] claims that the truth to be known is for the well-being of the knower."[27] Sapiential theology assumes the interconnectedness of the knowledge of God and the personal transformation of the knower. It is "engaged knowledge that emotionally connects the knower to the known."[28]

21. John Calvin, *Institutes of the Christian Religion*, ed. John T. McNeil, trans. Ford Lewis Battles (Philadelphia: Westminster, 1960), 1:7.
22. Ibid., 164.
23. John Frame, *The Doctrine of the Knowledge of*

Theology as Conversation and Proclamation — Lints, Thielicke

understanding, wisdom, and salvation, but also as a medium for entering into a dialogue with God Himself through His Word and the witness of His Spirit.

Proponents of this view will have to state what they mean by "conversation" or "encounter" so as to clearly delineate where this view stands in relation to, say, the existentialism of Bultmann. In what way does the Bible operate as a medium for dialogue? Is what the Bible "means" today, for example, connected essentially with what it meant to its original hearers?

What is the role of the Holy Spirit in this dialogue or encounter? Is it something akin to Calvin's "internal witness"? To Barth's existential application of the Word? Or is it similar to a charismatic Pentecostal's view of conversation with the Spirit? Can a theologian who has not "encountered" God truly, as a nonbeliever, still do theology on this view?

Modern proponents of this view would include Kierkegaard (probably the first Christian existentialist), who viewed the Bible as a love letter between God and the single individual, and possibly Karl Barth, who was much influenced by Kierkegaard. Barth approached theology as a dialogical engagement with God's revelation. He was dissatisfied with the current turn to theology as anthropology, so he focused on the transcendence and freedom of God and the normative authority of God's

What Is Theology?

Objective Theologies

Theology as Science (Rationality)	Theology as Search for Understanding/Wisdom	Theology as Ministry	Theology as Conversation and Proclamation
Hodge, Torrance, Warfield	Augustine, Migliore, Aquinas	Calvin, Frame	Lints, Thielicke

Theology as Science (Rationality):

and the natural sciences interact with and illuminate each other, and allow each other's distinctive characteristics to be appreciated, as an interesting means to the greater end of achieving at least a partial synthesis of their insights."[14] This proposal, he says, moves theology beyond the usual dialogue with philosophy, opening up interesting avenues for a public theology in a pluralistic world. McGrath has taken into account a new "settled" understanding of nature as itself an interpreted notion. This critical realist perspective McGrath applies to the examination of the data of theology.

4. B. B. Warfield, "The Idea of Systematic Theology," in *Studies in Theology*, vol. 9 of *The Works of Benjamin B. Warfield* (reprint, Grand Rapids: Baker, 1981), 56.
5. Ibid., 51.
6. Ibid.
7. Ibid., 57.
8. Ibid., 52.
9. Thomas F. Torrance, *Theology in Reconstruction* (Grand Rapids: Eerdmans, 1965), 9.
10. Thomas F. Torrance, *Reality and Scientific Theology* (Edinburgh: Scottish Academic Press, 1985), xiii.
11. Thomas F. Torrance, *Theological Science* (London: Oxford University Press, 1969), ix.
12. Ibid.
13. Cf. Alister McGrath, *A Scientific Theology* (Grand Rapids: Eerdmans, 2001).
14. Ibid., 3.

Theology as Ministry:

God (Phillipsburg, NJ: Presbyterian and Reformed, 1987), 79.

24. Ibid., 81.
25. Ellen T. Charry, *By the Renewing of Your Minds: The Pastoral Function of Christian Doctrine* (New York: Oxford University Press, 1997).
26. Ibid., 6.
27. Ibid., 7.
28. Ibid., 4.

Theology as Conversation and Proclamation:

revelation. His was a return to the theology of the Reformers in which the gospel of grace (and judgment) took pride of place. Theology and preaching were one for Barth, thus theology took the form of a prophetic address (an appropriation and articulation of God's speech in freedom, through His Word) to the church.[33] Lints and Thielicke would be contemporary representatives of this perspective.

29. Helmut Thielicke, *The Evangelical Faith*, 2 vols., trans. and ed. G. W. Bromiley (Grand Rapids: Eerdmans, 1974), 1:17.
30. Ibid., 23.
31. Ibid., 24.
32. Lints, *Fabric of Theology*, 59.
33. Cf. G. C. Berkhouwer's "The Voice of Karl Barth," in *A Half Century of Theology*, trans. and ed. Lewis B. Smedes (Grand Rapids: Eerdmans, 1977).

What Is Theology?

Subjective Theologies

Theology as Feeling (Description of)	Theology as Historical Science (or Scientific Method)	Theology as Transformation (Liberation) CCF	Theology as Negation (Radical Theologies)	Theology as Communal Language
Friedrich Schleiermacher	Adolph von Harnack	Gustavo Gutierrez, Rosemary Radford Ruether	Thomas J. J. Altizer, Jacques Derrida, Mark Taylor	Stanley Grenz, George Lindbeck, James McClendon Jr., Nancy Murphy
Friedrich Schleiermacher (1768–1834) sought to make the truths of the Christian religion more palatable to its "cultured despisers." He saw little essential disconnect between the truths of Christianity and the expressions of modern, secular culture. He wrote *The Christian Faith*, his dogmatics, in part with this apologetic task in mind. Yet Schleiermacher was intensely convinced that dogmatics be related to, and concerned with, the Christian church and with the spiritual life of the community of faith. In this sense, Schleiermacher's theology was oriented toward intentional ministry.	Adolph von Harnack (1851–1930) represented that branch of German theology known as "historicism," the school that prioritizes the historical and cultural "situatedness" of knowledge and belief. This does not mean that Harnack held no place for the transcendent in his theology, but the highest task of the historian (and theologian) is to identify that which is suprahistorical (transcendent) within the historical. This fits well with Harnack's understanding of the Christian religion as, "Eternal life in the midst of time, by the strength and under the eyes of God."[38]	Liberation theology begins its task in the context of lived experience—particularly the experience of the poor and oppressed. It focuses on Scripture's notion of the kingdom of God and seeks to implement its principles by "liberating, or setting free, social, economic, ethnic, and religious structures that are perceived to be oppressive."[40] Liberation theology in its various forms and contexts emphasizes the attention, compassion, and salvific action that Jesus showed to the poor, the oppressed, and the disenfranchised in His earthly ministry. Liberation theology is thus a "'new hermeneutic' for doing theology . . . arrived at by looking at the biblical texts from the perspective of the poor and oppressed."[41]	Negative or apophatic theology appropriates and extends the mystical approaches of Meister Eckhart and Dionysius the Areopogite, who were themselves influenced by neo-Platonic philosophy. Twentieth-century negative theology has much in common with streams of continental philosophy and literary criticism known as "deconstruction," which focuses on such concepts as "absence," "emptiness," and "difference."	George Lindbeck's groundbreaking book, *The Nature of Doctrine*, proposed an alternate course for theology in the waning influence of liberalism (which he labeled *experiential-expressivist theology*). He defines the task of descriptive theology (whether dogmatic or systematic) as that of giving "a normative explication of the meaning a religion has for its adherents."[56]
Schleiermacher also spoke of theology as a "science"; he recognized, however, the varied way in which all sciences, even the most "reputed," are interpreted, articulated, and related to one another. Given the complexity of defining dogmatics in and of itself, the first task, as Schleiermacher originally saw it, was to elucidate that reality to which dogmatics was essentially	The task of answering the question of "What is Christianity?" was for Harnack an exclusively historical task that of necessity must employ the methods of historical research. Unlike Schleiermacher, Harnack had no interest in combining this task with apologetics, for that would undermine the high standards of historiographical research. For Harnack, "What we are and what we possess, in any high sense,	Liberation theologies begin from the premise that traditional Christian theology has contributed to a dichotomizing of the search for truth and the significance of human existence and needs. Traditional theology has contributed more to the oppression of peoples than to the liberation	In its original form, negative theology simply emphasized God's transcendence and human fallibility, resulting in an essential inability to speak *positively* about God's essence and nature. The only way to attempt to draw closer to God or the knowledge of God is by using language to *unsay* who God is. Even classical theology depends on this strategy. We say that God is *not* finite, or He is *not* limited in His presence, or He is *not* limited in omniscience. "But we cannot say what he *is*, for that would be to put humanity in a position of objective knowledge over God's freedom and theology."[48]	Meaning is determined by the community of adherents to, and practitioners of, a specific language. In the same way, religions are defined by the doctrines they propose and to which participants adhere. Lindbeck anticipated Ludwig Wittgenstein in viewing language, not as verbal images that *picture* reality, but as a toolbox that *construes* reality, or assigns meanings to the various experiences, encounters, and things of life. Stanley Grenz, writing from an evangelical perspective, draws insights from postmodern epistemology, social theory, and linguistic philosophy in ways similar to that

What Is Theology?

Subjective Theologies

Theology as Feeling (Description of)	Theology as Historical Science (or Scientific Method)	Theology as Transformation (Liberation)	Theology as Negation (Radical Theologies)	Theology as Communal Language
Schleiermacher	Harnack	Gutierrez, Ruether	Altizer, Derrida, Taylor	Grenz, Lindbeck, McClendon, Murphy
related: the Christian church. Thus he would not ground his dogmatics on a "foundation of general principles," since the theology did not originate in the church. Nor would he seek to prove the correspondence of Christian faith and reason, because this would not, he suggested, add anything positive to the church that could not also be given to "every other society of faith or of life."[34] Rather, Schleiermacher grounded his dogmatics on what he perceived to be the "universal basis of all ecclesiastical communions," piety.[35] Piety he defined as the *"feeling (or immediate self-consciousness) of being absolutely dependent on, and in relation to, God."*[36] He defined theology (dogmatics) as: *"the science which systematizes the doctrine prevalent in a Christian Church at a given time."*[37] Doctrines, for Schleiermacher, were reflections of a Christian community that arose out of a particular, historically based experience of religious dependence. He did not want theology to be undertaken as *merely* a historical, or merely descriptive,	we possess from the past and by the past—only so much of it, of course, as has had results and makes its influence felt up to the present day. To acquire a sound knowledge of the past is the business and the duty not only of the historian but also of every one who wishes to make the wealth and the strength so gained his own."[39] The gospel, Harnack affirms, is a part of the past that cannot be replaced by anything else. It has past, present, and future repercussions unlike any other historical reality. Harnack's work (which was influenced by Albrecht Ritschl) opened the way for *historical Jesus* research. Much of this popular effort in theological circles of the continental Europe segment (see Albert Schweitzer) left little place for Harnack's concern for the suprahistorical element of the gospel. This concern was severely limited anyway by a fundamental, if unintentional, separation of kerygma (the essential gospel teaching/ preaching) from the actual events of history.	of the oppressed. But liberation is exactly what Jesus commended to His disciples. Liberation theologies (Latin American, feminist, black, etc.), then, view their task as that of modifying traditional theological symbols, metaphors, and interpretations (and introducing new ones) so theology can be a viable, useful instrument for liberation. Rosemary Radford Ruether, a feminist theologian, pronounced that theology no longer is a "science of a particular ecclesiastical tradition" or even of a particular faith, such as Christianity.[42] She sees the theologian as a generalist who can see "as his context and data the whole range of human sciences and the whole history of human cultures of self-symbolization."[43] The theologian must be fully aware of all aspects of human life and experience so that he can fully deal with the questions arising from the tension "between the 'is' and the 'ought' of the human life."[44] Theology should ultimately bring human existence into line with human aspirations. The traditional doctrines no longer *Man-centered theology*	Mark C. Taylor, a modern proponent of a form of negative theology or apophasis, writes, "There can be little doubt that theology is in disarray. Since the decline in the fortunes of Neo-orthodoxy, certainty about the nature and viability of the theological enterprise has waned. Absence of the Word has left theological voices either silent or confused. If theological language is again to be speakable and hearable, the sources of silence must be penetrated and the depths of confusion plumbed."[49] Taylor quotes Thomas Altizer, who says, "Little that is overtly theological is actually hearable or speakable today. However, this situation can make possible the realization of a new theological language, a theological language which will speak by way of the voice or the voices of our time."[50] Altizer is unhappy with theologies that attempt to correlate and accommodate to the questions and issues of their contemporary situation while trying to walk the line of orthodoxy. He claims such	of Lindbeck's *Nature of Doctrine.* He proposes that evangelical theology move beyond (noticing that in many ways it already has) foundationalism and ground theology in local, communal understandings, interpretations, and applications of Scripture. Theology is, Grenz says, the ongoing task of "meaning-making."[57] Drawing on anthropological studies on the nature of cultures, Grenz notes that cultures are the "outcome and product of social interaction"[58] Societies are groups of "social actors" who engage in the process of making meanings from the shared symbols and resources they possess and inhabit. Grenz states, "Theology is linked to the meaning-making activity found in all cultures. Evangelical theology, in turn, is related to the various symbols and activities in their function as building blocks and conveyers of the particular cultural meaning characteristic of evangelicals. To this end, theology engages with church practices, but more importantly it involves with the explication of the meaning of the symbols evangelicals

Subjective Theologies

Theology as Feeling (Description of)	Theology as Historical Science (or Scientific Method)	Theology as Transformation (Liberation)	Theology as Negation (Radical Theologies)	Theology as Communal Language
Schleiermacher	Harnack	Gutierrez, Ruether	Altizer, Derrida, Taylor	Grenz, Lindbeck, McClendon, Murphy

Theology as Feeling (Description of) — Schleiermacher

discipline. Indeed, he viewed apologetics as an essential task of the theologian. However, as a consequence of Schleiermacher's grounding of theology on the *feeling of absolute dependence* and of his view of doctrine as mere historically situated reflections of particular communities on the experience of their relation to God, Schleiermacher subjectivized religion. Theology became a kind of anthropology. He became the father of modern liberalism in which faith (piety) and knowledge (fact) were separated, so as to retain their value—but in distinct spheres.

34. F. D. E. Schleiermacher, *The Christian Faith*, 2d ed., ed. H. R. Mackintosh and J. S. Stewart (Edinburgh: T & T Clark, 1989), 3.
35. Ibid., 5.
36. Ibid., 12.
37. Ibid., 88.

Theology as Historical Science (or Scientific Method) — Harnack

This perspective is also taken, if in a somewhat different form, by German idealism, which had no little influence on Harnack's scientific-historical approach to the study of religion. G. W. F. Hegel, perhaps representing the height of idealist philosophy, viewed history as the outworking of the Spirit (*Geist*) in finite existence. The history of humanity is the story of the progression of life into higher modes of existence and understanding, made possible by the fuller realization of the Spirit (God) in the creation. His was a *panentheistic* (all the world is *in* God) theology, which was rationalistic in the sense that philosophy ultimately transcends theology and provides the clues to the meaning of the symbols and images given in theology. Thus the modern, enlightened world had a fuller grasp of ultimate reality than any other stage of history because the language of science and philosophy were providing articulate expressions of life's meaning and of God's existence and relation to the

Theology as Transformation (Liberation) — Gutierrez, Ruether

are recognized as providing the answers to ultimate questions. New answers must be brought to the great questions of life's meaning and value if people will be liberated to live out and represent fully the kingdom.

Gustavo Gutierrez, the prominent Latin American liberation theologian (who is credited as the founder of modern liberation theology), defines theology as "critical reflection on praxis."[45] Gutierrez uses the term *praxis* to mean the action of the church (preaching, sacraments, charity, service). Theology, in his view, *follows* praxis, as a second-order discipline. In this way Gutierrez proposes to redefine the common distinction between theology as wisdom and theology as rationality (science). Neither suffice, he claims, because both relegate the action of the church beneath the dignity and priority of the academic or contemplative theological life. Theology must be *critical*, he maintains, in that it draws on the resources of reason, church history, doctrine, and philosophy,

Theology as Negation (Radical Theologies) — Altizer, Derrida, Taylor

theologies (Tillich's, for example) should simply be honest and fully accept Nietzsche's declaration of the "death of God."

So Altizer: "A theology that chooses to meet our time, a theology that accepts the destiny of history, must first assess the theological significance of the death of God. We must realize that the death of God is an historical event, that God has died in our cosmos, in our history, in our *Existenz*."[51]

Theology must fully dissociate itself from the church and its creeds, rites, symbols, and doctrines. Western theology, Altizer claims, is hopelessly linked to ontology. The Christian view of God, for example, is a fusion of the biblical worldview with Greek metaphysics.[52]

Theology, then, must be "alienated from the Church," and can be neither "kerygmatic, apologetic, or dogmatic," for it to find its own voice. The task of theology is "the discovery of its own ground." It must find this ground through experiencing its own *dark night of the soul*, seeking solace neither in

Theology as Communal Language — Grenz, Lindbeck, McClendon, Murphy

share . . . Evangelical theologians attempt to set forth their understanding of the particular 'web of significance,' 'matrix of meaning,' or 'mosaic of beliefs' that lies at the heart of the evangelical community."[59] After this postmodern, postfoundationalist turn in the theological situation, Grenz notes, evangelical theology takes on the characteristic of being local—tied to specific communal representations of evangelicalism within the broader camp: "No longer can any one group, tradition, or subnarrative claim without reservation and qualification that their particular doctrinal perspective determines the whole of evangelicalism."[60] Theology takes on the form of a "never-ending conversation about the meaning . . . of the symbols that as evangelicals they are committed to maintaining and that form the carriers of meaning for all."[61]

James McClendon Jr., who is similarly optimistic about the task of a postfoundationalist theology, writes that theology is "contextual."[62] McClendon disagrees with Karl Rahner, who sees theology as "attempting to conform ever more

What Is Theology?

Subjective Theologies

Theology as Feeling (Description of)	Theology as Historical Science (or Scientific Method)	Theology as Transformation (Liberation)	Theology as Negation (Radical Theologies)	Theology as Communal Language
Schleiermacher	Harnack	Gutierrez, Ruether	Altizer, Derrida, Taylor	Grenz, Lindbeck, McClendon, Murphy
	world. Theology, then, was ultimately subservient to philosophy, thought it was not without meaning and significance in the sphere of religion itself. 38. Adolph von Harnack, *What Is Christianity?* trans. Thomas Bailey Saunders (reprint, New York: Harper & Brothers, 1957), 8. 39. Ibid., 4.	but it should be subservient to praxis. It is *action*, not contemplation or doctrine, that maintains the kingdom of God in human history. Thus, for Gutierrez, theology takes the subjective (and anthropological) turn: "Theology must be man's critical reflection on himself, on his own basic principles. Only with this approach will theology be a serious discourse, aware of itself, in full possession of its conceptual elements."[46] This does not mean that his theology has no place for an objective element (such as authoritative revelation). For Gutierrez, the Word of God speaks to the church. The church acts (or fails to act) upon that word in faith. Theology is the critical, reflective task of discerning *how* that action is taking place . . . or *whether* it is taking place as it should. Theology asks the question: *Is the church transforming the world and "building a new, just, and fraternal society"?*[47] 40. J. David Turner, *An Introduction to Liberation Theology* (New York:	"prayer or meditation." As he says, "theology can know neither grace nor salvation; for a time it must dwell in darkness, existing on this side of the resurrection. Consequently, the theologian must exist outside of the church: he can neither proclaim the Word, celebrate the sacraments, nor rejoice in the presence of the Holy Spirit . . . it must first exist in silence."[53] Blending his deconstruction and its signature notion of *differance* with negative theology, Jacques Derrida ultimately criticizes the latter as simply a negative way to emerge with the same kind of positive language as any other form of theology or of speaking.[54] Derrida is faced with the inevitable difficulty in speaking of negative theology: Is not speaking of negative theology itself a positive use of language? Derrida puts it well: "Is there ever anything other than a 'negative theology' of 'negative theology'?"[55] Only deconstruction, Derrida maintains, can enable a genuine nonsaying and thus not fall	closely to 'the true theology' —to theology as *God knows* it ought to be."[63] For McClendon, "our theologies must represent us as we are, as well as representing God as God. That fact introduces a contextual, not a sinful, pluralism into the theological task." This is not a mere subjectivism, McClendon notes, because the content of theological reflection within local communities is always the gospel. Further, reflection on this content is also the means by which mutual criticism and "witness" takes place within Christian communities.[64] Nancy Murphy suggests that theology take a more holistic direction. Taking as her starting point the postmodern conception of language as a *doing* more than as a *picturing*, she suggests that theology must attend not only to the biblical text as a foundation, but to the experience of the individual and community who are interpreting that text. Thus theology has objective dimensions as well as subjective dimensions, and both must be held together. The

Subjective Theologies

Theology as Feeling (Description of)	Theology as Historical Science (or Scientific Method)	Theology as Transformation (Liberation)	Theology as Negation (Radical Theologies)	Theology as Communal Language
Schleiermacher	Harnack	Gutierrez, Ruether	Altizer, Derrida, Taylor	Grenz, Lindbeck, McClendon, Murphy
			prey to onto-theology and the metaphysics of presence.	lens for understanding, interpreting, and reading, however, is always one's local, cultural, and communal situation. This is why this theology is considered *more* subjective than objective.

University Press of America, 1994),
1. See also, *The Politics of Latin American Liberation Theology*, ed. Richard L. Rubenstein and John K. Roth (Washington, DC: Institute Press, 1988).
41. Ibid.
42. Rosemary Radford Ruether, "Foundations for a Theology of Liberation," in *Liberation Theology* (New York: Paulist, 1972), 2.
43. Ibid., 3.
44. Ibid.
45. Gustavo Gutierrez, *A Theology of Liberation*, ed. and trans. C. Inda and J. Eagleson (Maryknoll, NY: Orbis, 1973), 6.
46. Ibid., 11.
47. Ibid., 15.

48. Cf. Jacques Derrida, "How to Avoid Speaking: Denials," in *Derrida and Negative Theology*, ed. Harold Coward and Toby Foshay (New York: State University of New York Press, 1992). Originally printed in *Languages of the Unsayable: The Play of Negativity in Literature and Literary Theory*, ed. Stanford Budick and Wolfgang Iser (New York: Columbia University Press, 1989). See also *Silence and the Word: Negative Theology and Incarnation*, ed. Oliver Davies and Denys Turner (Cambridge: Cambridge University Press, 2002).
49. Mark C. Taylor, *Deconstructing Theology* (New York: Crossroad, 1982), 45.
50. Cited in Taylor's *Deconstructing Theology*. The quote is originally from Thomas J. J. Altizer, *The Self-Embodiment of God* (New York: Harper and Row, 1977), 3–4.
51. Thomas J.J. Altizer, "America and the Future of Theology," in *Radical Theology and the Death of God*, ed. Thomas J. J. Altizer and William

56. George Lindbeck, *The Nature of Doctrine: Religion and Theology in a Postliberal Age* (Philadelphia: Westminster, 1984).
57. Stanley J. Grenz, *Renewing the Center: Evangelical Theology in a Post-Theological Era* (Grand Rapids: Baker, 2000), 180.
58. Grenz is referring here to the definition given by Anthony P. Cohen in *Self Consciousness: An Alternative Anthopology of Identity* (London: Routledge, 1994), 118–19.
59. Ibid., 181.
60. Ibid.
61. Ibid.
62. James Wm. McClendon, *Ethics: Systematic Theology*, rev. ed. (Nashville: Abingdon, 2002), 1:35.
63. Ibid.
64. Ibid.

What Is Theology?

Subjective Theologies

Theology as Feeling (Description of)	Theology as Historical Science (or Scientific Method)	Theology as Transformation (Liberation)	Theology as Negation (Radical Theologies)	Theology as Communal Language
Schleiermacher	Harnack	Gutierrez, Ruether	Altizer, Derrida, Taylor	Grenz, Lindbeck, McClendon, Murphy

Hamilton (Indianapolis: Bobbs-Merrill, 1966), 11.
52. Ibid., 12.
53. Ibid., 15.
54. For a discussion of this point, see *God, the Gift, and Postmodernism*, ed. John D. Caputo and Michael J. Scanlon (Bloomington, IN: Indiana University Press, 1999).
55. Ibid., 83.

PART TWO
The Possibility of Systematic Theology

Introductory Considerations

The discipline of *systematic theology* has long contributed an essential approach to theological work. Systematics has enjoyed various levels of priority, and sometimes high prominence, among the related fields of historical theology, biblical theology, practical theology, and philosophical theology. Some practitioners of theology have held that biblical theology is best suited to represent divinely revealed truth (so G. Vos), while others have asserted that only systematics can apply the results of exegesis or of biblical theology in a way that is most beneficial for contemporary Christians. These theologians would argue that it is one thing to discover and articulate what Paul said about justification, for example, but quite another to show how Paul's teachings coalesce with input from James in a systematic theology of justification. This contributes even more broadly to a systematic theology of salvation.

However, in the postmodern context, systematic theology is viewed with skepticism as to its intrinsic ability to offer anything productive to pluralistic intellectual and social life. In the "hermeneutics of suspicion," all forms of knowledge and established systems of knowledge are viewed as embedded in a historical context. They are seen as so context bound that they cannot speak transcendently from within that context. We live in a pluralistic society—religiously pluralist, ideologically pluralist, politically pluralist, and ethnically pluralist. In such a context, what would be the hope for an overarching *systematic theology*? At best one might hope for systematic *theologies*. Furthermore, the Bible itself contains diversity and plurality along with its qualities of unity and sameness. Theologians such as Hans Frei and George Lindbeck have advocated a purely narrative approach to theology, which limits its content to the intrinsic narrative structure and conceptual content of Scripture's language.

More severe warnings issue from those who perceive a tendency for intellectual or political elites to lust for control; these thinkers have inferred that "systematic theology" or "dogmatics" leads to, and is in fact derived from, an unhealthy desire by religious elites to control the flow of information, belief, and power over those who adhere to their arbitrarily determined "metanarratives."

For theologians sensitive to the postmodern critique, systematic theology might still be a viable and necessary option for theology, but they would take under advisement the warning that their theological systems must not arise out of sinful idolatry. Theologians are challenged to rethink their biases or presuppositions. In this latter sense, postmodernity can offer a healthy corrective to the ongoing task of theological formulation. Thus, systematic theology is a necessary and important opportunity for theological reflection in which a logical conceptual order—if not imposed violently from outside Scripture and its concepts—organizes the content of Scripture's assertions. In authentic systematics, a contemporary application or significance is sought through the meaning of the scriptural texts. The purpose is to learn more about God through the observation and experience of being human in the world God has created.

The Possibility of Systematic Theology

Different Perspectives on the Possibility

Systematic Theology Is Possible but Should Be Tied to Biblical Theology	Systematic Theology Is Possible Because Doctrines Are Necessary	Systematic Theology ("Dogmatics") Is Possible and Necessary Because of Scripture's Diversity
D. A. Carson	Louis Berkhof	Emil Brunner
D. A. Carson carefully argues for the possibility of a systematic theology that is based on the authority and contents of the entire Bible, taking into account Scripture's unity and diversity—its whole and its parts. He defines systematic theology as "the branch of theology that seeks to elaborate the whole and the parts of Scripture, demonstrating their logical (rather than merely historical) connections and taking full cognizance of the history of doctrine and the contemporary intellectual climate and categories and queries while finding its sole ultimate authority in the Scriptures themselves, rightly interpreted."[1] Biblical theology then is "that branch of theology whose concern it is to study each corpus of the Scripture in its own right, especially with respect to its place in the history of God's unfolding revelation."[2]

Biblical theology can provide a coherent formulation of Paul's theology or Peter's theology. Even so, Carson points out, biblical theology may yet "fail to find the consensus needed for systematic theology." Granted that a systematic theology is possible, however, something Carson affirms, "biblical theology itself achieves new dignity, for one entailment of the systematic theology would be the certainty that the contributing corpuses are coherent if rightly organized in the historical framework of biblical theology."[3]

Carson offers several reasons why a theologian can optimistically attempt to formulate a systematic theology from his exegesis and understanding of the New Testament: (1) Everyone already has a systematic theology (even atheists). Carson means that everyone has a worldview regarding ultimate reality, a "core belief system," in which one aims for "maximal logical consistency."[4] (2) "The data base to be urged | In his *Systematic Theology*, Reformed theologian Louis Berkhof distinguishes between "dogma" and "doctrines," suggesting that the dogma comprises "those statements or formulations of doctrines which are regarded as established truths by the body of Christians which formulated them, and which are therefore clothed with authority."[10] Berkhof writes that dogmas are essential for true Christianity, since church life and the lives of Christians are guided by the authority of Holy Scripture. The Bible presents the revelation of God as absolute truth and the unity of the church is dependent on the agreement of essential doctrinal understanding. For Berkhof, dogmatics "deals with the doctrinal truth of Scripture in a systematic way, and more particularly with that truth as it is confessed by the church. It studies the doctrine of the church as a whole, and considers each article of faith in its relation to the whole. As such it is not only scriptural, though it must be this first of all, but also bears an ecclesiastical imprint."[11]

Berkhof, appealing to the Reformed tradition of systematic theology, notes that the task of dogmatics is "to set forth in scientific form absolutely valid truth, and to embrace the entirety of Christian doctrine (Hodge). . . . It seeks to give a systematic presentation of all the doctrinal truths of the Christian religion. It may not rest satisfied with a description of what was at one time the content of the faith of the Church, but must aim at absolute or ideal truth. It is not a purely historical or descriptive science, but one that has normative significance."[12]

Berkhof suggests that the first phase of dogmatics must be the constructive task, in which the theologian "deals primarily with the dogmas embodied in the confession of his Church, and seeks to combine them into a systematic whole."[13] | Emil Brunner, one of the so-called "crisis theologians" along with Karl Barth and Rudolf Bultmann, wrote that God's truth, when it is received by frail humanity, is "refracted" into a multiplicity of perspectives.[17] This was true for the apostles (and thus for writers of the Bible) as well as for us today. Dogmatics (the science of theology) is the church's necessary task of seeking out the centrality and unity of God's divine truth. Dogmatics deal with the historicity of Scripture and the diversity of the biblical writings as its results describe the truth that the church professes.

Brunner deals with four objections to the need for dogmatics as an intellectual discipline. The first two objections concern the intellectualizing of Christianity, stealing its vitality. Second, theology as a mere intellectual exercise can displace and undermine the "simplicity of faith" as well as the Bible's call of the disciple to action.[18] The third possible objection is that dogmatics can lead to ecclesial authoritarianism, and thus to a "system of doctrinal coercion, which is in opposition to the freedom of faith."[19]

The fourth objection, Brunner explains, is that dogmatic theology can make the task of apologetics more difficult, rather than easier, because it can make the gospel less rather than more clear with its intellectual labors.[20]

In response to these possible objections to the necessity of systematic theology, Brunner writes of three "urgent necessities for dogmatics which spring from the life of the church itself, and cannot be ignored."[21]

First, the church needs theology because it continually engages in a "struggle against false doctrine." Christian systematic theology enables the church to discern true doctrinal belief |

Different Perspectives on the Possibility

Systematic Theology Is Possible but Should Be Tied to Biblical Theology	Systematic Theology Is Possible Because Doctrines Are Necessary	Systematic Theology ("Dogmatics") Is Possible and Necessary Because of Scripture's Diversity
Carson	Berkhof	Brunner
upon systematic theologians is the entire Bible, the canonical sixty-six books."[5] (3) Scripture presents a "progressive, and thus historical, nature of God's unfolding revelation to his people throughout the course of biblical and redemptive history." The coherence of the biblical story suggests that coherent implications may be drawn in reference to that story. (4) While diversity exists in the New Testament regarding its pastoral concerns, this does not undermine its basic doctrinal ("creedal") unity.[6] (5) Much of the New Testament's diversity can be attributed to "the diverse personal interests and idiosyncratic styles of the individual writers."[7] (6) "On the basis of these reflections it must be insisted that there is no intrinsic disgrace to theological harmonization, which is of the essence of systematic theology."[8] (7) Carson offers a concluding suggestion for systematic theologians, that they "should be careful to note how various truths and arguments function in Scripture and they should be very cautious about stepping outside those functions with new ones."[9]	This task, Berkhof says, requires "more than a logical arrangement" of the truths named in a church's confession: "Many truths that are merely stated in general terms must be formulated; the connecting links between the separate dogmas must be discovered and supplied and formulated in such a way that the organic connection of the various dogmas becomes clear; and new lines of development must be suggested, which are in harmony with the theological structure of the past."[14] This approach, Berkhof says, must be distinguished from that of Schleiermacher, Troeltsch, and Barth, drawing primarily on the revelation of Scripture rather than "religious experience or faith (Schleiermacher, Ritschl, Kaftan, Schaeder), nor on history (Troeltsch), nor on church proclamation (Barth)."[15] In its systematizing task, Berkhof states, dogmatics should not rest content with describing the various doctrines and their relation to the whole; rather, the theologian should show how the doctrines that he professes and describes systematically are "absolute truth," deriving as they do through a kind of scientific method from Scripture. The theologian should also, Berkhof suggests, approach his system with a degree of criticism, recognizing that theology can err in its proposals and conclusions.[16]	from error, or even heresy. Second, the church needs systematic theology to disciple its adherents in the knowledge of the content of the faith. Christianity's content must be "thought out afresh and reformulated in intellectual terms"[22] for this to occur. Third, systematic theology is necessary for the task of biblical exegesis. One cannot rest content, Brunner explains, in the mere awareness of "what the apostle Paul means by the 'righteousness of God' in a particular passage in the Epistle to the Romans; we want to know what he means by this expression as a whole, and also how this specifically Pauline phrase is related to other phrases which, although they sound different, contain a similar meaning in other biblical writers."[23] Brunner points to the diversity of the theology of the Bible to conclude for the necessity of systematic theology. Dogmatics helps us to understand the truth of God's revelation in a unified way. Through systematic reflection on the scriptural text, the theologian can see back through the refractions of light to the source and content of God's truth more clearly if the task of theology is done well.

1. D. A. Carson, "Unity and Diversity in the New Testament: The Possibility of Systematic Theology," in *Scripture and Truth*, ed. D. A. Carson and John Woodbridge (Grand Rapids: Baker, 1992), 69–70.
2. Ibid., 69.
3. Ibid., 71.
4. Ibid., 77.
5. Ibid., 79.
6. Ibid., 88.
7. Ibid., 89.
8. Ibid., 90.
9. Ibid., 93.

10. Louis Berkhof, *Systematic Theology* (reprint, Grand Rapids: Eerdmans, 1996), 18.
11. Ibid., 35.
12. Ibid., 58.
13. Ibid.
14. Ibid.
15. Ibid.
16. Ibid., 59.

17. Emil Brunner, "The Necessity for Dogmatics," in *The Christian Doctrine of God*, trans. Olive Wyon (Philadelphia: Westminster, 1950), cited in *The Necessity of Systematic Theology*, 2d ed. ed. John Jefferson Davis (Grand Rapids: Baker, 1978), 75–84.
18. Ibid., 76.
19. Ibid., 77.
20. Ibid., 78.
21. Ibid., 79.
22. Ibid., 80.
23. Ibid., 81.

The Possibility of Systematic Theology

Different Perspectives on the Possibility

Systematic Theology Is Possible and Necessary Because of the Unity of Scripture's Story	Systematic Theology Is Possible, but Always Contextual	Systematic Theology Is Possible, but Always Hermeneutical
Richard Lints	David Clark	David Tracy
Richard Lints, in an article in *Modern Reformation*, responds to a postmodern aversion to "thinking systematically about theology." He says that this negative perception of systematic theology derives from a twofold challenge in the societal mapping of contemporary religion: (1) the plurality of religions and thus the multiplicity of "sacred" texts, and (2) in Christianity itself, the plurality of interpretations (readings) of the Bible.[24]

Lints, describing the "pluralist impulse and the loss of systematic theology," laments of postmodern approaches to interpreting Scripture (in particular the approach of David Tracy). He complains that they provide no transcendent criterion for adjudicating whether interpretations of Scripture are correct. According to Lints, "These postmoderns view the Bible as just one possible way of interpreting things, a way that displays certain profound truths about human communities, but a way that can and ought to be corrected by the diverse insights of different communities."[25] The authority of the Bible suffers under the weight of a multiplicity of conflicting (but equally valid) interpretations.[26]

For Lints, the proper theological approach to Scripture and its interpretation is to allow Scripture to supply the reader with its own set of interpretative criteria, with its own "framework of meaning and interpretation." Then the reader can allow all of Scripture (not just parts of it in isolation from other parts) to furnish the interpretive lens. Lints says, the Bible must be seen "as a world that is to be inhabited or as a story in which our lives are to be understood."[27] It is possible to read Scripture as a unified story of redemption, because Scripture originates with a divine Author, as God's | David Clark, in a recent book on theological prolegomena, writes of the importance to evangelical theology of maintaining a proper dual emphasis on the subjective (contextual, experiential) and objective (kerygmatic, scriptural) poles of theological considerations. Upon discussing the model of theology as inductive science, propounded by Charles Hodge and B. B. Warfield, Clark notes that the model proves to be insufficient for doing systematic theology for three reasons: (1) It implies that, because order in a discipline is preferable to disorder, "systematic theology is superior to Scripture." This implication fails to recognize that the Bible "already possesses a certain coherence of its own." It is not "an incoherent jumble that awaits a coherence that only theology gives."[31] (2) "The model of theology as inductive science does not properly consider the context of theological work."[32] Context, Clark points out, includes the theologian's personal, cultural, religious context. Also, one must realize that the theologian's approach to analyzing the "data" of Scripture involves interpretation from the outset. There are no uninterpreted facts. "The inductive model . . . does not include in its structure a place for these choosing, organizing, correlating, and testing functions. It does not adequately recognize the theologian's methodological, philosophical, cultural and personal assumptions, his blind spots, biases, or interests."[33]

Nonetheless, Clark upholds the importance and necessity of systematic theology, while affirming "a deep loyalty to biblical revelation as the controlling principle of theology," and recognizing "the value of contemporary contexts."[34] Clark discusses the dialogical interrelation between | Roman Catholic theologian David Tracy, in *The Analogical Imagination: Christian Theology and the Culture of Pluralism*,[38] suggests that three primary branches of theology fit a pluralistic context: (1) fundamental theology, (2) systematic theology, and (3) practical theology. The three branches of theology correspond, each in some measure, although with overlap, to the three "publics" of academy (fundamental theology), church (systematic theology), and society (practical theology). All theology in a pluralistic world should seek a measure of publicness, avoiding a merely sectarian result that is unable to speak to issues of the larger world. Each theology will achieve a degree of publicness in relation to the structure of the society with which it is intimately involved. For theology to be *both* theological and public, each of which are necessary aspects of theology, it must be theocentric, Tracy asserts.[39]

Systematic theology has as its sphere of "publicness" the church, for systematic theologies are "church theologies." Tracy writes that "the systematic theologian's major task is the reinterpretation of the tradition for the present situation."[40] Thus the systematic theologian should demand that any representative theology derives from within the practice of his particular confessional tradition. Faith and theology are wed for the systematician. Reinterpretation, for Tracy, does not mean a simple restatement of a faith's fundamental beliefs. That kind of repetitional theology ("authoritarian, dogmatist, fundamentalist"),[41] Tracy claims, is more ideology than actual theology.

A truly public systematic theology for Tracy is possible if the theologian approaches the task as a kind of "hermeneutical |

Different Perspectives on the Possibility

Systematic Theology Is Possible and Necessary Because of the Unity of Scripture's Story	Systematic Theology Is Possible, but Always Contextual	Systematic Theology Is Possible, but Always Hermeneutical
Lints	Clark	Tracy

Word. Thus, "the Scriptures contain their own principles of organization as they narrate the past, present, and future of this history as well as its meaning as God's creations and re-creation."[28]

Systematic theology, then, "mirrors" the story of redemption, the organizing principle, of the Bible. But it does so with a different emphasis from that of biblical theology. Systematic theology examines the themes and concepts of Scripture from the perspective of the Bible as a "completed whole," rather than analyzing these themes merely chronologically and thus limited to theologizing from a particular, limited historical period.

Systematic theology should reflect the "unity of redemption," though it should not ignore the "organic and ironic character of that unity across time."[29] As for the possibility of doing systematic theology in a postmodern climate, Lints concludes, "It is thus neither arrogant nor intolerant to affirm that there is one final, systematic theology, as long as that theology faithfully represents the God who created and now re-creates human beings in his own image. At the same time, it is naive and dangerous to assume that just any theology can fulfill that function. Only systematic theology that is tethered to the theology of the Scriptures that God has authorized will faithfully represent him."[30]

24. Richard Lints, "Thinking Systematically About Theology," *Modern Reformation* 12, no. 1 (January/February 2003): 23. See also Michael Horton, "Who Needs Systematic Theology When We Have the Bible?" *Modern Reformation* 12, no. 1 (January/February 2003): 13–22.

biblical theology (or exegesis) and systematic theology. Systematic theology, Clark writes, has an interpretive role. The theologian does not simply reiterate the biblical text, nor should the theologian simplistically seek to apply every text without reference to the author's intention, which itself is always cloaked in cultural garb (a worldview, a language, differing situations, etc.). Theology should pay attention to the task of "principalizing," which is a process of "abstracting from the Bible certain general theological truths."[35] Systematic theology seeks to discern transcultural truths and apply them in a new cultural situation. Clark notes the potential dangers involved in such an approach. It may be difficult, first of all, to discern the transcultural in a given biblical text. Also, this interpretive approach could encourage a theologian to usurp the Bible's authority by his or her own cultural, political, or ideological interests.

Nonetheless, the systematic theologian should seek to "summarize, interpret, and apply" biblical truth to "express Christian truth in certain ways, but then always tie our thoughts back to the authoritative words of the Bible for critique."[36] The goal of evangelical theology, Clark writes, "is biblically controlled and contextually relevant knowledge that leads to spiritual wisdom."[37]

31. David K. Clark, *To Know and Love God* (Wheaton, IL: Crossway, 2003), 50.
32. Ibid.
33. Ibid., 51.
34. Ibid., 57.
35. Ibid., 91.

theology." The theologian bears the responsibility of interpreting faithfully but creatively the primary religious text of the tradition. The turn to hermeneutics in theology is, of course, strongly suggestive of the post-Enlightenment, and post-Kantian recognition of humanity's historical and communal situatedness and embeddedness: "The surest mark of contemporary systematic theology is precisely a profound acceptance of finitude and historicity."[42] The systematic theologian must be a member of a particular religious community, in which he or she "risks faith" in the tradition, and "has the right and responsibility to be 'formed' by that tradition and community."[43]

Systematic theology can truly be a fruitful discipline, Tracy asserts, if the religious text under interpretation is a religious "classic." By "classic," he means "those texts, events, images, persons, rituals and symbols which are assumed to disclose permanent possibilities of meaning and truth."[44] The theologian interprets the classic for the public of the church and interacts with that classic on the model of a "disclosure," always being open to new meanings in differing situations and contexts.

To treat a religious text as a religious classic is to eschew an authoritarian appeal to the universal validity of that classic's authority, and to the theologian's conclusions as universally valid and binding over other classics and interpretations. "All theological claims to the formulation of universal truth must be put under the strictly theological hermeneutics of suspicion of 'idolatry.'"[45] This "suspicion of idolatry" is formulated in Tracy's earlier work, *Plurality and Ambiguity*, as the condition of postmodernity, which he greatly respects:

The Possibility of Systematic Theology

Different Perspectives on the Possibility

Systematic Theology Is Possible and Necessary Because of the Unity of Scripture's Story	Systematic Theology Is Possible, but Always Contextual	Systematic Theology Is Possible, but Always Hermeneutical
Lints	Clark	Tracy
25. Ibid. 24 26. Ibid. 27. Ibid., 25. 28. Ibid. 29. Ibid., 32. 30. Ibid.	36. Ibid., 97. 37. Ibid., 98.	"Postmodernity demands multiple discourses for interpretation itself. As postmodern writers and thinkers remind us, we live within intertextuality. Texts and methods of interpretation often conflict. They may even attempt to annihilate one another. . . . We can trust ourselves to a conversation with the classics with this provisio: we admit that everything—ourselves, our texts, and the conversation itself—is deeply affected by the ambiguity and plurality that touch all. . . . There is no innocent interpretation, no innocent interpreter, no innocent text."[46] "As reflection on Ultimate Reality, and thereby on the limit questions of our existence, theological interpretation, like all interpretation, is a precarious mode of inquiry. Theologians can never claim certainty but, at best, highly tentative relative adequacy. Theologians cannot escape the same plurality and ambiguity that affect all discourse."[47] --- 38. David Tracy, *The Analogical Imagination: Christian Theology and the Culture of Pluralism* (New York: Crossroad, 2000). 39. Ibid., 52. 40. Ibid., 64. 41. Ibid., 99. 42. Ibid., 100. 43. Ibid., 67. 44. Ibid., 68. 45. Ibid., 66. 46. Ibid., 78–79. 47. Ibid., 84–85.

Contemporary Challenges to the Possibility of Systematic Theology

J. I. Packer has written that contemporary "revisionists," as he calls them, "insist that, whatever else the biblical tradition can do for us, it cannot give us objective knowledge of God—conceptions, that is, that are guaranteed true because God himself is vouching for them."[48] Modern academic scholarship has sought from the origins of biblical criticism to invalidate any claim that Scripture has normative, transcendent authority. The point of literary interpretations all the way to textual deconstruction is to seek to unmask the "ideologues" and liberate the oppressed reader from a world in which the text of the Bible corresponds with the way things actually are.

Packer gives the postmodernist conclusion: "So theology should give up its proud claim to be stewarding and safeguarding universal truth and settle instead for the humbler role of describing religious phenomena from a standpoint of universal cultural relativism. . . . Theology must adjust to the fact that we have no word from God in any ordinary, natural, specifiable sense."[49] There is no final, fixed, authoritative word from God in transcribed, written form. Theologians, then, the revisionists assert, must find their task in creative solutions to modern problems, to providing meaning in a chaotic, meaningless world, or to simply describing the religious sentiments of a bygone historical people.

For some theologians this is a welcome turn toward freedom of expression. For others it is a trend to be resisted only in its extreme forms, i.e., in those radical theologians who discount the merits of tradition. Is there a responsibility among theologians to translate or transpose the truths of theology into a postmodern key? In its mediated, nuanced forms, postmodernism can provide a helpful corrective to unhealthy theological dogmatism and linguistic idolatry, but this corrective must be carefully evaluated lest it deny the theologian, and the church, access to a word from God continued in the Scriptures, relating to knowable truths.

---

48. J. I. Packer, "Is Systematic Theology a Mirage? An Introductory Discussion," in *Doing Theology in Today's World,* ed. John Woodbridge and Thomas Edward McComiskey (Grand Rapids: Zondervan, 1991), 19–20.
49. Ibid.

35

The Possibility of Systematic Theology

Contemporary Challenges to the Possibility of Systematic Theology

Constructive, Revisionist Theology	"Poetic" Theology, Not Dogmatic, Systematic Theology
Rosemary Radford Ruether	Don Cupitt

Rosemary Radford Ruether

Rosemary Radford Ruether, a leader in contemporary feminist theology, writes expressly in of her perceived responsibility to "reinterpret" the "biblical prophetic tradition." Such reinterpretation is nothing new, Ruether writes, and is rooted in the Enlightenment tradition: "Feminism reinterprets the biblical and Christian egalitarian tradition in terms of the modern consciousness of social systems as human artifacts, not divine orders of nature. It takes original equality to be the foundational truth of human nature in the light of which patriarchy can and must be transformed. It recontextualizes this tradition in terms of the problematic of female subjugation and emancipation."[50]

For feminism, as well as for theologies that are related by a similar hermeneutical impulse (such as liberation theology), the task of theology cannot be limited to a simple restatement of ancient meanings tied to their primary forms of expression with no regard to current understandings of human life and nature and to current concerns for equality, equal rights, ecological responsibility, etc. The plain sense of a scriptural text, especially if taken in isolation from larger thrusts of meaning, may lack a certain ability to speak meaningfully to contemporary issues. Ruether writes, "Feminist theology calls for a comprehensive effort to express the whole system of theology as mutual interrelation. . . . In terms of anthropology this would mean affirming that both men and women possess the fullness of human nature. They do not relate to each other as superior to inferior or as complementary parts of human nature in which each has the half that the other lacks. Rather, woman as woman and man as man each possess the fullness of human nature. . . . Our God-language must also reflect this understanding of Christ and ourselves."[51]

The strand of repeated, uncritical appropriation of the patriarchal imagery and male headship language within Christianity cries out for a rethinking of biblical interpretation and a reinterpretation of the meaning of Scripture with attention to new, more culturally sensitive metaphors, cast in gender neutral dress. This recasting of language should apply not only to how we understand humanity, as equal whether male or female, but to how we understand the Godhead: "If all persons, female and male, are fully human, mutually interrelated, then God cannot be imaged in terms of only one gender. God is beyond gender; neither male nor female, and the ground of mutual personhood of both men and women. . . . If women are as fully the image of God as men, then God must be imaged in metaphors drawn from female being and activity as much as from that of males. But this female imaging of God should not reinforce unjust gender stereotyping. Rather, it should point us to the redeemed fullness of personhood of both women and men."[52]

Don Cupitt

Don Cupitt, a leading postmodern theologian, wrote an article, "Post-Christianity," in which he states his preference for "poetic theology" over dogmatic religion.[53] Cupitt thinks that very little of what counts as philosophically true beliefs in dogmatic religious systems can actually be proven as such. Religious, dogmatic beliefs function, rather, as "badges of membership," for religious groups that serve to distinguish communities and provide controls for self-identity.[54] Dogmatic theology is "non-rational," and "works by the 'logic of difference': it includes by excluding, encourages hostility and (to an astonishing degree) inhibits thought. . . . It puts a brake on thinking, as Wittgenstein used to say."[55]

Cupitt thinks that the history of Western dogmatic theology is a story of the religious elite who have employed metaphors to "fiction themselves" into positions of power and to exploit "the idea that ordinary humans are benighted sinners who need to be rescued from their plight by an elect group of supernaturally-accredited religious professionals."[56]

In the sphere of philosophical truth-value, theology simply just does not bring anything to the table. It can only provide benefit by way of negativity: showing that it cannot answer the questions that it never needed to raise in the first place, because "There is only the stream of language-formed events . . . nothing is hidden. Everything can be put into words. When everything lies open to view, there is nothing left to be explained."[57]

Cupitt concludes that the function of poetic theology, in contrast to dogmatic theology, is to "embellish our life," not to provide information that cannot save us in the first place: "We may therefore reinterpret Christian doctrines as being a sacred poetry of divine love, love that takes human form in Christ, love that is entirely content to burn, burn out and pass away. When we really have come to understand that this life and this world are coextensive and completely outsideless—when we see that this world is wholly *our* world—then we may become capable of what I have called 'ecstatic immanence,' and 'glory.'"[58]

In an earlier book, *Taking Leave of God*, Cupitt suggested that the "religious man of the future" might be the one who is able to step away from the heteronomy and dogmaticism of traditional religious faith and to assert autonomy and critical stance toward dogmatic, ideological, Christian tradition.[59] Cupitt asserts that the Christian faith can be practiced with piety and effectuality apart from unquestioning belief in "Christian supernatural doctrines."[60] Such a person would view the whole Bible much in the same way, Cupitt suggests, as Christians viewed the Old Testament—as an inherited deposit and resource for faith, but yet something to be surpassed in this modern age.[61]

Contemporary Challenges to the Possibility of Systematic Theology

Constructive, Revisionist Theology	"Poetic" Theology, Not Dogmatic, Systematic Theology
Ruether	Cupitt
Such recasting of traditional biblical language is not unfaithful to the biblical tradition, Ruether asserts, because all language about God is metaphorical, not literal. This opens up a vast space of freedom in reinterpretation and recontextualization in light of contemporary concerns and issues. 50. Rosemary Radford Ruether, "The Task of Feminist Theology," in *Doing Theology in Today's World*, 373–74. 51. Ibid. 52. Ibid.	53. Don Cupitt, "Post-Christianity," in *Religion, Modernity and Postmodernity*, ed. Paul Heelas (Oxford: Blackwell, 1998). 54. Ibid., 226–27. 55. Ibid., 227. 56. Ibid. 57. Ibid., 228. 58. Ibid. 59. Don Cupitt, preface to *Taking Leave of God* (New York: Crossroad, 1981). 60. Ibid. 61. Ibid.

PART THREE
Four Divisions of Theology

Four Divisions of Theology

Systematic Theology	Biblical Theology	Historical Theology	Philosophical Theology
Systematic theology is that discipline of theology that seeks to be comprehensive, logical, and unified in its description and presentation of biblical revelation, with particular attention to how God's special revelation can be applied to the contemporary situation. Biblical theology tends to focus on biblical events (such as the progress of redemption) and stories chronologically, exegetically, and thematically. Systematic theology emphasizes concepts, such as the doctrines of God, humanity, sin, the person and work of Christ (salvation), heaven and hell, the nature of the church, eschatology (the end times), and how the significance of these concepts for the Christian life can be explained. The primary source material for systematic theology is the Bible, both Old and New Testaments. Secondary source material is also consulted from church history, historical theology (including creeds and confessions), philosophy, and all other areas of learning (science, sociology, psychology, etc.). Anything that bears on the topic or concept being explored can contribute. The best kind of systematic theology is that which integrates other kinds of theology (and other kinds of thought). Theology should be grounded firmly in biblical exegesis and consistently mediated and illuminated by historical and philosophical theology. Some theologians and theological departments have dropped the adjective *systematic* in favor of other terms, such as *constructive* or *contemporary*. This terminology emphasizes a normative aspect of theology: its purpose is not merely to "systematize" in an abstract, descriptive sense, but to bring theological insights to bear on current issues of life and society. It can	Biblical theology is that discipline of theology which follows closely the story lines and themes of Scripture while exegeting (drawing *out of*) and presenting the meaning of the biblical text for a contemporary audience. Often biblical theology will focus on a particular book, e.g., *the theology of Romans*, or on a particular writer, e.g., *the theology of Paul*. It may also be subdivided into two disciplines: Old Testament theology and New Testament theology. As a theological discipline, however, biblical theology has usually focused on the unity of the two Testaments, while recognizing points of disunity, plurality, or discontinuity. Biblical theology often focuses on what the text *meant* (historically/chronologically) to its original audience more than, though not exclusive to, what it *means* to contemporary readers. Geerhardus Vos rightly points out, however, that the biblical theologian, no less than systematic theology, also "transforms," or presents in fresh ways, the material of Scripture, because the biblical theologian does not simply restate exactly what the Bible says. The difference, he says, is the "principle" upon which their theology occurs: historical (in BT) versus logical (in ST).[1] Biblical theology seeks to follow the progression of redemption and of revelation in the Bible and to understand the Bible on its own terms: in its own concepts and its own culture.[2] Johann Gabler is well known for establishing the unique discipline of biblical theology as distinct from systematic, or dogmatic, theology. He feared that the increasing rationalism and skepticism that accompanied post-Reformation Enlightenment theology was undermining the significance and power of the biblical text. Biblical	Historical theology describes the development of theology over the two thousand years of the Christian church and—at least for some historical theologians—seeks to appropriate for contemporary discussions insights gained from this study. The historical theologian can focus on periods (e.g., Patristic, Medieval, Reformation, Modern) or on particular theologians (e.g., Augustine, Aquinas, Luther, Calvin, Barth). Geoffrey Bromiley, a historical theologian, has suggested there are two valid aims for historical theology. The first is the objective and descriptive approach in which the historical theologian is primarily a *historian*: "It views the ideas of Christians in the first instance as a branch of the intellectual history of the race."[5] The second approach is more of an "apologetic," in which the theologian "adopts a positive attitude, drawing attention to the great achievements of Christian thinkers and stressing their formative role in intellectual history." This approach is as much *theological as historical*. Historical theology is useful to both systematic and biblical theologies, because we do not do theology in a historical vacuum. We live and think in specific social, cultural, and theological settings. Historical theology reminds us of this reality by giving us insights into how people of other settings and ages have understood biblical revelation. It broadens our range of possible interpretations of Scripture as well as our understanding of humanity. Theologians of the past have had particular insights into Scripture and the world that theologians of the present may not have. Also, Christianity is a historical religion, developing over time. We owe a debt to the	*Philosophical theology* employs the resources of philosophy (logic, reasoning, critical thinking, and the humanities) to seek new angles on the theological task. If the primary source material of systematic and biblical theology is special revelation, the Bible, it might be the case that the primary source material of philosophical theology is general revelation—human reason, in particular. This does not mean that philosophical theology does not, or should not, view Scripture. But philosophical theology may seek to answer questions that the Bible may neither ask or answer. At its best, it will do so by invoking Christian wisdom from within a Christian life view to try to make sense of difficult and important life issues. When does life begin? Why would God create hell? Why do innocent people suffer? What is the nature of reality? Philosophical theology should not neglect the primary source material of Scripture, but it can derive *implications* from Scripture that go beyond the typical concerns of systematic, biblical, or historical theologies. Philosophical theology usually can be broken down into several categories: *ethics* (how are we to live?), *metaphysics* (what is the nature of reality?), *epistemology* (how do we know what we know and how do we justify our beliefs?), and *hermeneutics/philosophy of language* (how does language and speech provide mediate truth and meaning?). Over the years, theologians have viewed the benefits of theology quite differently. Tertullian asked the famous question, "What does Jerusalem (Christian theology) have to do with Athens (pagan philosophy)?" Luther probably was correct that philosophy should be viewed and practiced as a "handmaiden" to

Four Divisions of Theology

Systematic Theology	Biblical Theology	Historical Theology	Philosophical Theology
also denote a turn from authority to open-ended creativity. The postmodern preference for local, communal "language games" rather than for timeless, biblical "metanarratives" would be better served by a term like *constructive* rather than *systematic*.	theology has since taken numerous forms, and has recently made another comeback. Theologians have recognized that we neglect the redemptive-historical context of biblical texts to our peril. Some, such as Vos, think that biblical theology is superior to systematic theology in its ability to study the "actual self-disclosures of God in time and space."[3] D. A. Carson takes a more moderate position when he says that biblical theology "mediates the influence of biblical exegesis on systematic theology."[4] Regardless, the best kind of biblical theology is that which does not dichotomize "what it meant" from "what it means" such that its contemporary significance becomes irrelevant to the discussion. 1. Geerhardus Vos, *Biblical Theology: Old and New Testaments* (Grand Rapids: Eerdmans, 1954), 23. 2. Gerhard F. Hasel, *Evangelical Dictionary of Theology*, ed. Walter Elwell (Grand Rapids: Baker, 1984), 164. 3. Vos, *Biblical Theology*, 13. 4. D. A. Carson, "The Role of Exegesis in Systematic Theology," in *Doing Theology in Today's World*, ed. John D. Woodbridge and Thomas Edward McComiskey (Grand Rapids: Zondervan, 1991). 66.	thinkers and leaders of our history, and a treasure trove of theological understandings therein. A basic knowledge of the creeds and confessions throughout the history of the church, for instance, is a necessary enterprise for any kind of theologian. Richard Muller, a prominent church historian of the Reformation period, makes the sobering but important point that all theology becomes historical once it has come off the printing press![6] 5. Geoffrey Bromiley, *Historical Theology: An Introduction* (Edinburgh: T & T Clark, 1994), xxiv. 6. Richard Muller, "The Role of Church History in the Study of Systematic Theology," in *Doing Theology in Today's World*, 80.	theology. It is widely understood now, however, that theology cannot, nor should, escape the influence and use of philosophy. The question is not, *should* theologians use philosophy, but *how should theologians use it appropriately* to serve theology and the church?

PART FOUR
The Nature of Doctrine

Introductory Issues

Since the beginnings of the Christian church and the work of Paul and other apostles, theologians have spoken of God's revelation in Scripture in terms of "doctrines." They used Scripture in nontheological areas of worship and life, as the increased attention to genre considerations in systematic theology attests. But doctrine or "teaching" has always carried with it the connotations of authority regarding Christian life (ethics, action, lifestyle, etc.) and belief. Doctrine can teach both *what* should be believed—content—and *how* that content should be used in understanding, applying, and actualizing faith. Paul, in his first letter to Timothy, said: "Watch your life and doctrine closely. Persevere in them, because if you do, you will save both yourself and your hearers" (4:16). Doctrine and life go together.

Doctrines do not spring automatically off the texts of Scripture, however, unmediated by interpretation and systematization. They are results of the theological interpretation of Scripture in real historical contexts. The Chalcedonian and Nicene creeds, for example, which define the nature of the Trinitarian relationship within the Godhead and the two natures of Christ, were the results of sustained—and often confrontational—reflection on Scripture. They emerged out of a strongly felt need to differentiate right and wrong theological interpretations of biblical texts regarding the nature of God, Christ, and the relationships between the Godhead. Doctrine is the teaching of Scripture, interpreted and reiterated within the historically and socially conditioned community of faith.

Theologians have approached the issue of the nature of doctrine individually. Some emphasize the authoritative source of doctrine (for Protestants, Scripture; for Catholics, both Scripture and the ecclesiastical tradition that mediates/interprets it) and are optimistic about the ability to derive, understand, and maintain stability in doctrinal formulations (e.g., once a doctrine, always a doctrine—even though that doctrine will require fresh understandings that fit changes in situation and life). This does not mean that doctrines must be considered in purely cognitive or intellectual form. It does mean that doctrines are the stuff of life, provided by Scripture in its diverse literary forms. Doctrines provide Bible readers with the content and the context for living as Christian disciples.

Other theologians emphasize the historical and cultural aspect of doctrinal formulations, over against their unchanging universal, transcendent quality. They point out that because doctrines are interpreted, formulated, and expounded by fallible individuals within fallible communities, doctrinal formulation is more expressive of human fallibility than it is of divine, transcendent truth. Though doctrines develop within human communities over time, they are continuing reflections on real events and true disclosures that demand sustained interpretation and application. The extreme form of this view, seen in some corners of modern liberalism, holds that doctrines do not refer to any extralinguistic or extrahistorical reality; they are simply the sociologically conditioned and historically situated attempts of religiously oriented people to make sense of and provide meaning for life. We are not considering this view in our discussion here.

Finally, some theologians emphasize the local (not necessarily historical) and communal formulations of doctrines. Such work looks at attempts by communities to understand and apply Scripture within a setting.

We present three approaches to the nature of doctrine. One emphasizes the cultural-linguistic turn in theology (Lindbeck); one emphasizes the canonical nature of Scripture and its present and ongoing authority for the Christian life and church (Vanhoozer). The third emphasizes the historical development of doctrine as serious but ultimately limited reflection on the authoritative text of Scripture (McGrath).

The Nature of Doctrine

Approaches to Doctrine

The Postliberal Cultural-Linguistic Approach	The Postconservative Canonical-Linguistic Approach	The Genesis of Doctrine and a "Scientific Theology"
George Lindbeck	Kevin Vanhoozer	Alister McGrath

The Postliberal Cultural-Linguistic Approach — George Lindbeck

George Lindbeck's *The Nature of Doctrine* perceives three current "types" of conceiving the nature of doctrine. The first emphasizes the "cognitive aspects of religion," in which doctrines "function as informative propositions or truth claims about objective realities."[1] The second approach is the "experiential-expressive" approach to religion and doctrine, which views doctrine as "noninformative and nondiscursive symbols of inner feelings, attitudes, or existential orientations."[2] Lindbeck sees Friedrich Schleiermacher, the "father of modern liberalism," as beginning this emphasis on religious experience and "feeling."

Lindbeck himself proposes a third approach, a "postliberal way of conceiving religion and religious doctrine."[3] He is intrigued by the ecumenical theological context in which adherents to once-opposed dogmatic traditions (e.g., Catholics and Lutherans) now in some settings dialogue with little conflict as such between their respective doctrines. This connection is possible although the understanding of the doctrines themselves has not changed. What caused the shift in mindset, which enables such an ecumenical approach while retaining doctrines that previously served as borders not to be crossed? What kind of approach to religion and doctrine can enable such a current ecumenical situation, without one or more dogmatic parties capitulating to the doctrinal expectations or requirements of the other? Lindbeck draws on Wittgenstein's influence in the philosophy of language, in which "meanings" in any language are tied to their use in that specific language, to propose the "cultural-linguistic" approach to doctrine and religion. Religions, on this view, resemble grammar. Doctrines resemble languages. Lindbeck states, "The function of church doctrines that becomes most prominent in this perspective is their use, not as expressive

The Postconservative Canonical-Linguistic Approach — Kevin Vanhoozer

Kevin Vanhoozer proposes an alternative conception of doctrine to George Lindbeck's "cultural-linguistic," postliberal model. Vanhoozer's postconservative, "canonical-linguistic" approach defines Christian doctrine as "direction for the church's fitting participation in the drama of redemption."[8] Doctrine is the "way of truth" and the "stuff of life." Doctrine is meant to be lived out by Christians in the community of faith, not merely cognitively or intellectually understood. Doctrine, when rightly understood and applied to life, influences one's intellectual life (propositional information), and in fact all aspects of the self as a Christian disciple.

Vanhoozer lists four contemporary options for the location of divine revelation, all of which, he notes, give a place for the Bible: (1) biblical propositions (e.g., conservative evangelicalism), (2) the person of Christ (e.g., Barth), (3) Christian piety (e.g., Schleiermacher), and (4) church practices (Lindbeck and the "cultural-linguistic turn"). The Bible's authority for theology, Vanhoozer notes, differs with each of these views. It is either "co-extensive with revelation" (conservative evangelicalism), a "witness to revelation" (Barthianism), "an expression of one's experience of revelation" (Schleiermacher), "or a product and condensation of the church's language and life" (the cultural-linguistic turn).

Vanhoozer asserts that Lindbeck's proposal, in which he locates authority, not in the biblical text but in the church—each particular ecclesial "culture"—effectively replaces the authority of Scripture with tradition. The Reformation doctrine of *Sola Scriptura* gets lost. Vanhoozer finds a better approach in what Nicholas Wolterstorff has called "divine authorial discourse."[9]

This approach, Vanhoozer explains, encourages the reader to attend to the literary forms as well as the content of the

The Genesis of Doctrine and a "Scientific Theology" — Alister McGrath

Alister McGrath, a historical theologian of note, writes of the importance of the role of history and tradition in the formulation and expression of doctrine, in his study *The Genesis of Doctrine*.[13] Theology, like all interpretative paradigms, including the scientific, is tradition dependent. Doctrines emerge posterior to the initial, historical Christ-event and are communal responses to that event. McGrath emphasizes that theological and doctrinal reflection are subsequent to, but reliant on, the historical reality of God's redemptive and revelatory activity. Part of the ongoing task of theology is a kind of self-reflection, the criticism of present theological understandings of Scripture. This willingness to criticize and to return reflectively to the biblical text enables major shifts in doctrinal understanding and the attempt to be faithful to the scriptural text, the origin of doctrine.

McGrath emphasizes the importance of the careful attention to the diversity of Scripture's forms, emphasizing especially its narratives:

"The narrative possesses an interpretive substructure, hinting at doctrinal affirmations."

"On the basis of these scriptural hints, markers and signposts, doctrinal affirmations must be made which are then employed as a conceptual framework for the interpretation of the narrative."[14]

McGrath, in his three-volume *A Scientific Theology*,[15] explores the possibilities and dangers of an interdisciplinary approach to theology, which critically appropriates the methods of science in order to relate the insights of science to a broader public (apologetics). He clarifies the task and results of theological inquiry with the benefits of scientific understanding.

In the second volume of this series, McGrath discusses

Approaches to Doctrine

The Postliberal Cultural-Linguistic Approach	The Postconservative Canonical-Linguistic Approach	The Genesis of Doctrine and a "Scientific Theology"
Lindbeck	Vanhoozer	McGrath

Lindbeck

symbols or as truth claims, but as communally authoritative rules of discourse, attitude and action."[4]

Lindbeck says that church doctrine has a regulative function like that of a language's grammar. This conceptualization of doctrine as providing "rules" for theological discourse within a particular and distinct community of faith (religion, denomination, or local church) enables various denominations to reconcile "without capitulation." Rules are binding only in certain circumstances and locations. Lindbeck illustrates thusly: "The rules, 'drive on the left' and 'drive on the right' are unequivocal in meaning and unequivocally opposed, yet both may be binding: one in Britain and the other in the United States, or one when traffic is normal and the other when a collision must be avoided. Thus oppositions between rules can in some instances be resolved, not by altering one or both of them, but by specifying when or where they apply, or by stipulating which of the competing directives take precedence."[5]

To complete the analogy, Lindbeck suggests that doctrinal debates that once must have been irreconcilable due to the historical-social situation can now be "harmonized by appropriate specifications of their respective domains, uses, and priorities."[6]

Doctrines are regulative, for Lindbeck's proposal, and in fact are *only* regulative, serving a function, or functions, within particular communities of faith. As such, "doctrines do not make first-order truth claims." This assertion, Lindbeck notes, sets him apart from the long tradition of those who appealed to the "rule of faith" in discerning doctrinal teachings from Scripture and in making theological proposals from that basis.[7]

---

1. George Lindbeck, *The Nature of Doctrine: Religion and Theology in a Postliberal Age* (Philadelphia: Westminster, 1984), 16.

Vanhoozer

divine discourse, employing the imagination and reason. The use of Scripture as the way of truth and the stuff of life means that it is not only doctrine in the form of propositions with which theology should be concerned. Rather, the church can "appreciate the diversity of Scripture's genres," so we do not have to "choose between the Bible's truth and its affective power." On this view, doctrine regains its significance as an "indispensable cognitive and imaginative instrument for shaping the life of the church."[10] The task of theology turns from being merely the use and acquisition of theory and knowledge to being a way of *wisdom*, the stuff of life. This view, Vanhoozer notes, overcomes the "theory/practice dichotomy." Because the subject matter of theology is "Jesus Christ . . . the way, the truth and the life," theology "must deal with truth, with ways of living, and with the meaning of life."[11]

The metaphor of the theater and actor exemplifies this holistic approach to theology and theological interpretation of Scripture. Doctrine insists on, and enables audience participation in, the action of the Godhead. The relation of the church to Scripture, on this view, is that of the "performance of the gospel" to the "script of the gospel." Vanhoozer presents the canonical-linguistic model to theologians "for its turn to practice, for its emphasis on wisdom, and for its creative retrieval of the principle of *sola scriptura*. . . . Canonical-linguistic theology attends both to the drama *in* the text—what God is doing in the world through Christ—and to the drama that continues in the church as God uses the Scriptures to address, edify, and confront its readers."[12]

---

8. Kevin J. Vanhoozer, *The Drama of Doctrine: A Canonical-linguistic Approach to Christian Theology* (Louisville: Westminster-John Knox, 2005).

McGrath

Lindbeck's proposal in *The Nature of Doctrine* and faults the insufficient attention it gives to the realism of Christian theology. Theology must refer meaningfully to realities independent of thought and reflection. The postliberal view also fails to take into account the development of Christian doctrine in its extralinguistic qualities. Lindbeck offers no component of reflecting critically on theological and doctrinal development within various historical periods and ecclesial communities. "The Christian idiom cannot simply be taken as 'given': it must be interrogated concerning its historical and theological credentials."[16] McGrath argues that theology must take into account the historical development of doctrine, so that some of that development can be "recognized as inappropriate and inauthentic, and revised or removed in the course of an ongoing theological reflection."[17]

For McGrath, Lindbeck's linguistic approach fails to bring theology into the open marketplace of ideas in a pluralistic world. McGrath thinks that an interdisciplinary conversation between the methods and concerns of science and the methods and concerns of theology offers a possibility for a public theology based on a critical-realist ontology. The theologian can acknowledge the limitations of historical and social context (and thus the limitations of point of view) while recognizing that everyone else is dealing with those same limitations. But this should not stop the theologian from seeking to understand, analyze, and describe reality.

---

13. Alister McGrath, *The Genesis of Doctrine: A Study in the Foundation of Doctrinal Criticism* (Oxford: Blackwell, 1990).
14. Ibid., 60.
15. McGrath, *A Scientific Theology*.
16. Ibid., 50.
17. Ibid.

The Nature of Doctrine

Approaches to Doctrine

The Postliberal Cultural-Linguistic Approach	The Postconservative Canonical-Linguistic Approach	The Genesis of Doctrine and a "Scientific Theology"
Lindbeck	Vanhoozer	McGrath

9. Cf. Nicholas Wolterstorff, *Divine Discourse: Philosophical Reflections on the Claim That God Speaks* (Cambridge, MA: Cambridge University Press, 1995).
10. Vanhoozer, *Drama*, Introduction.
11. Ibid.
12. Ibid.

2. Ibid.
3. Ibid., 7.
4. Ibid., 18.
5. Ibid.
6. Ibid.
7. As Alister McGrath points out in *A Scientific Theology* (Grand Rapids: Eerdmans, 2001), 48, some "postliberals" wish to distinguish themselves from Lindbeck's clear "antirealism." For this, see T. R. Philips and D. L. Okholm, eds., *The Nature of Confession: Evangelicals and Postliberals in Conversation* (Downers Grove, IL: InterVarsity Press, 1996), 69–80.

PART FIVE
The Nature of Divine Revelation

What Is Revelation and Where Is It Located?

Revelation means "disclosure." It is based on the Greek word *apokalypsis*, from which we get "apocalypse."[1] The "Apocalypse (Revelation) of St. John" is God's unveiling of ultimate reality (The Lord *is* on the throne) and eschatology (God *will be* victorious over evil and Satan in the final days of history). This is not, however, the only way in which the term revelation is used in theology. The broad usage of the term is "the disclosure by God of truths at which people could not arrive without divine initiative and enabling."[2] Thus the concept *revelation* encompasses and denotes a whole host of questions and issues regarding how God makes Himself and the truth of divine things known to humanity. How does God "unveil," or "reveal," saving truth to humankind in order to redeem them? Why has He disclosed Himself to humanity? To what extent does God make Himself known through His creation? Does He reveal Himself immediately to humans (e.g., through direct, mystical encounters or heightened consciousness)? Or does He use mediate sources and instruments (e.g., the Bible, the preached gospel, nature) to reveal Himself and the truth about Him?

The Roman Catholic theologian Avery Dulles has written an insightful and classic text, *Models of Revelation,*[3] in which he provides several models to describe how theologians have understood the nature and locus of revelation. As it would be difficult to improve on his fivefold categorization, we will use those categories, but with some modifications, deletions, and additions to fit the flow of the surrounding charts.

---

1. Colin Brown, ed., *New International Dictionary of New Testament Theology* (Grand Rapids: Zondervan, 1971), 310.
2. T. Desmond Alexander and Brian S. Rosner, eds., *New Dictionary of Biblical Theology* (Downers Grove, IL: InterVarsity Press, 2000), 732.
3. Avery Dulles, *Models of Revelation,* 2d ed. (Maryknoll, NY: Orbis, 1994).

Charts *on* Prolegomena

The Nature of Divine Revelation

Five Models of Revelation

Revelation as Speech	Revelation as History	Revelation as Dialectical Presence

Revelation as Speech

Avery Dulles prefers the term "revelation as doctrine" as more precise. We have chosen the broader term *speech*. Essentially this view sees revelation as being the spoken word(s) of God to humanity. God has been seen fit to use linguistic communication to provide salvific, historical, and ontological (nature of being) information about Himself, humanity's sinful state, and the way He has determined to bring about the redemption of humanity and creation.

This word can take place through a variety of means, depending on the particular perspective: either through the written words of Scripture, the spoken words of God in human history (which later became Scripture), a combination of both, or through the "oracles" of God spoken through the church (cf. Dulles).

Protestants traditionally have focused on the written and spoken words of God as found in the texts of canonical Scripture (commonly known as the "Scripture principle"). Many evangelical theologians in the modern period, Carl F. H. Henry for example, have defended the primarily propositional content of revelation, as given in Scripture. Propositions, as derived from the text, are statements of fact or truth that correspond to reality, either present (as in the indicative), desired (as in the imperative), or future (as in prophetic literature)—to the extent that the propositions are clearly and truly expressed. So propositions are doctrines that state what is actually the case.

Revelation in the evangelical sense, according to Henry, "takes propositional form and conveys universally shareable information. . . . The meaning of words is clear only in logical or propositional context, and not above, behind or under this."[4] Henry is a staunch adherent and apologist of the "plenary verbal" view of the inspiration of Scripture, that *all* the words of Scripture were directly inspired of God. Revelation is tied directly and inseparably from the written form of the Word of God in the Bible. Henry saw in the modern (technological, scientific, journalistic) situation a "crisis of truth and

Revelation as History

The *revelation as history* model arose in large part from the theological turn to biblical theology in the mid-twentieth-century, a focus on God's redemptive acts in history rather than on God's revelation through written word. The written word (Scripture) is the testimony to God's actions. But, according to biblical theologians such as William Temple and G. Ernest Wright, the actions/events must be seen as having revelatory priority over the witness to the acts.[10] God reveals Himself primarily through His great deeds done in the course of history, notably in biblical history. The Bible and church teachings are witnesses to revelation, but revelation itself is not equated with that witness.

Revelation is God's self-manifestation through historical events as He interacts redemptively and creatively with humanity and the created order. Biblical theologians such as Wright and Oscar Cullmann posited two lines of history: ordinary history and sacred history. Sacred history, *heilsgeschichte*, is the heart of God's revelation. Scholars such as Wolfhart Pannenberg and Ernst Troeltsch criticized this dichotomizing of the sacred and the ordinary for its withdrawal of the acts of God in history into the local sphere of faith, "unjustifiably removed from the probings of historical criticism."[11]

John Baillie suggests that revelation involves not merely receiving "information by communication," but that in revelation God actually gives Himself in communion. He wrote that "God reveals himself *in action*—in the gracious activity by which he invades the field of human experience and human history which is otherwise a vain show, empty and drained of meaning."[12] The Bible, Baillie notes, is "essentially the story of the acts of God"; it is not so much a collection of oracles or timeless propositions as it is "a record of what God has done."[13]

For Wright, "history is the chief medium of revelation," and "biblical theology is the confessional recital of the redemptive acts of God in a particular history." Wright titled

Revelation as Dialectical Presence

Emil Brunner, with Karl Barth, reacted against both German higher criticism and Hegelian idealism. In German higher criticism the Bible became so historicized that it lost all transcendent meaning and significance. In German idealism, G. W. F. Hegel's philosophizing of religion, the historical reality and present significance of a God-relationship with Christ was swallowed up into nothingness by human rationality. Brunner did not want to locate revelation as simply the outworking of the World-Spirit in human history and appropriated by pure thought (so Hegel) or in a mere enlightening of the consciousness by the divine presence. Rather, taking sin, evil, and human finitude into account, Brunner located revelation in an encounter of God with humanity, which occurs in the historical Christ-event, but which is mediated in the present as a spiritual encounter of faith. He states, "The being of man as person depends not on his thought but on his responsibility, upon the fact that a supreme Self calls to him and communicates Himself to him. It depends on . . . 'responsive actuality,' the claim of the Self who is Lord that is at the same time the assurance of the graciously creating and justifying Self, as it is perceived in faith."[19]

Brunner says that man has being, not in his rationality, but in the outworking of his response to this encounter of God's presence. His deepest nature consists in this "answerability," i.e., in this existence in the Word of the Creator.[20] To know God, Brunner says, is not only to *know* the truth, but to *be in the truth*. Truth is founded in the historical event of the incarnation of God in Christ, which enables us to be *in the truth* as we apprehend that truth by faith. Truth is, further, a "communicative word." "It is the self-communication of the true Thou without which we cannot be true selves."[21]

The Bible, for Brunner, is an indispensable witness to the truth of God's reality and inbreaking presence to humanity in the encounter of subject with subject, I with Thou. The Word of God is the personal being of God as present in Christ, speaking love to the human heart and initiating new

52

Five Models of Revelation

Revelation as Speech	Revelation as History	Revelation as Dialectical Presence

Revelation as Speech

word'' in which God's special revelation has been supplanted and superceded by a society that has forgotten the God of the Bible. God has been seen fit to preserve His special revelation in the form of a written text. Thus Christians are, in a very real sense, a "people of the book" because their view of God, of themselves, and of their relation to God is utterly dependent on the authority of this written communication. This is not to suggest, however, that the *events* of God's redemption throughout history were not also revelatory and meaningful, nor even that one cannot speak of revelation occurring *in* history through God speaking to the prophets, apostles, and Bible writers. But *what* is revelatory in these redemptive events is given in propositional form. Statements of words in the form of doctrine, or history, or poetry disclose God's nature, being, and reality. Revelation, in terms of directly inspired words from God to man, ceased with the closing of the canon. The deposit of God's revelation is the Scriptures of the Old and New Testaments. Christians have the privilege of turning to this book to hear God's revelation and the responsibility to share the content of that revelation with those who have no access to it. As Henry states, "Before the modern era the Christian community would unhesitatingly have answered the query 'What has God revealed?' by the response 'What the inspired writers teach.'' The writers themselves understood revelation that way, and so did Jesus Christ.[6] Henry and other propositionalists defend the cognitive and verbal elements of revelation in the face of a trend toward Scripture as symbolic, mythological, and experiential.

Some evangelical theologians have advocated the inspired nature of the biblical text by focusing more on the linguistic and literary diversity in the biblical text. On this view the Bible is a divine and human, completed speech-act that bears its message through a variety of communicative mediums— not just propositions meant to teach cognitively doctrinal truths.[7]

Kevin J. Vanhoozer, for example, has been instrumental in

Revelation as History

his book on the subject *God Who Acts*, in response to the then common term, "God Who Speaks." Wright was proclaiming that the Bible is not just the "Word," but it is primarily an account of the "Acts" of God in history as interpreted by those who so experienced God. For Wright, contemporary Christians can enter into the biblical story and derive its meaning by an act of *recital*, in which the redemption described in biblical history becomes a part of one's contemporary experience through memory. Wright saw the locus of revelation as occurring primarily and first in the objective, historical events recorded in Scripture. Derivatively, revelation may occur inwardly, "in the inner consciousness of man, . . . yet the nature and content of this inner revelation is determined by the outward, objective happenings of history in which individuals are called to participate."[15]

Cullmann is well known for his use of the term "salvation history" (*heilsgeschichte*). He viewed God's revelation as the inbreaking of God in Christ uniquely in human history at a point in time, as if a vertical line became perpendicular to a horizontal line, but from which point the horizontal line (human history) became utterly transformed, both backward and forward. Events seen from a human standpoint, then, must be interpreted from the perspective of the Christ-event and God's redemption of creation. "Meanings" in events are not self-authenticating or self-evident; rather events become meaningful when viewed from the perspective of faith and when interpreted by the biblical authors.[16]

Ernst Troeltsch, dealing with the difficult question of the relation between faith and history, argued that faith is dependent on history. Faith does not relate only to a supernatural history, such as that posited by Cullmann, Wright, and others. Faith is dependent on the interpreter's understanding of the history that bears religious significance personally and in the faith community. The nature of faith, Troeltsch argues, includes the necessity to connect the object of one's faith and belief with history. This means, however, that Christianity

Revelation as Dialectical Presence

life and authentic personhood in those who are encountered by it. Revelation (the truth) is not something *we* can possess; rather it "lays hold of us."[22]

Eschewing the possibility of a natural revelation, Barth, also a "dialectical theologian," declared that revelation is "the event of God's sovereign initiative."[23] Revelation is, as such, God Himself acting freely in the incarnation and redemptive act of Jesus Christ at a decisive moment in history. This revelation was witnessed to by the apostles, with this witness being preserved in the writings of Scripture. Christians today are called upon to respond to the witness of Scripture and to the encounter of God's revelation by the communal, ecclesiastical practice of *confession*.

Rudolf Bultmann famously departed from Barth at various points regarding the issue of revelation and of the interpretation of that revelation. Both agreed that revelation is received in a dialectical encounter of man with the Word of God, in the various forms that that "Word" takes. In ways similar to that of the Barth-Brunner debate on the question of whether there is a natural "point of contact" for divine revelation in the person, Barth and Bultmann differed on the question of the locus of the authority of revelation in the revelatory encounter. As Donald Bloesch points out, for Barth the basis of revelation's authority "is outside us (*extra nos*) in the objective self-revelation of God in Jesus Christ." For Bultmann, however, it is "the experience of the new life, the realization of forgiveness that is impressed upon us in our encounter with the preached word of the cross."[24]

Bultmann is known for his "existential theology," in which the Christ of faith is distinct from the Christ of history (Jesus). He thus "demythologized" the New Testament to make room for faith in a modern, scientific world. Yet Christ still speaks, as the Christ of faith, through that revelation to those who interpret it existentially. All interpretation of revelation, Bultmann asserts, is interpretation with presuppositions. Interpretation without presuppositions is not possible. The most

Five Models of Revelation

The Nature of Divine Revelation

Revelation as Speech	Revelation as History	Revelation as Dialectical Presence
bringing speech-act theory to the fore in theological hermeneutics with *Is There a Meaning in This Text?*[8] Vanhoozer has supplemented the view of revelation as "speech" in its primarily propositional emphasis with a broader, genre-inclusive understanding of revelation. On this view, revelation is not simply understood as "cognitive" and "doctrinal," in which the divinely inspired words of Scripture must correspond exactly with the reality they signify. Rather, Vanhoozer takes into account the insights of literary theory and speech-act philosophy to show that words do not *simply* refer. Words also *perform* a variety of actions. Speech is the result of an *action* of a communicative agent who desires to achieve a result by his or her activity of speaking. "The category *speech act* acknowledges that saying too is a doing, and that persons can do many things by saying."[9] Thus, through the Bible, God does more than just communicate propositional truths (though He does that). The form of the individual and various types of literature in the Bible are not incidental to their meaning. Rather, the forms contribute to their meanings because meaning cannot be divorced from authorial intent—or, better, from what the author was *attending to* in his writing. Not all of Scripture is limited to cognition, then, in the sense Carl Henry would suggest with his emphasis on its propositional content.	should be studied as a historical phenomenon, "subject to the same principles of historical inquiry as any other discipline."[17] Admittedly this will open up very difficult problems for faith. How can Christianity, for instance, claim epistemic superiority over other religions when history is so vast and so all-encompassing? Nonetheless, Troeltsch says there is an "essential and inseparable connection of faith with history and the necessity of a religious view of history. From time to time, it may well be necessary to relax these historical connections and to make room for one's own religious creativity. But, basically, innovations will hardly be more than new positions regarding history and new fruitful applications of what was already given. To abandon history would be tantamount to faith's abandoning itself and settling for the fleeting and trivial religious stirrings produced by a subjectivity left to its own resources."[18]	objective interpretation of revelation, then, according to Bultmann, is done by those who are most *subjectively* and *existentially* interested in the religious significance of the revelation. "Only those who are stirred by the question of their own existence can hear the claim which the text makes."[25] The "crisis" theologians Bultmann, Barth, and Brunner emphasized the dialectical encounter of revelation. God's freedom means that His revelatory acts are not tied to a written text or even to historical events. Rather, God encounters people in a variety of ways to make His reality known. Barth emphasized the transcendent nature of God in this encounter, whereas Bultmann and Brunner emphasized God's immanence and the capability of humanity to receive His revelation existentially. Bloesch appropriates many of Barth's insights regarding the dual reality of the hidden and revelatory aspects of God in his evangelical dialectical theology.[26] Bloesch's theology is an emphasis on the unity of "Word and Spirit" (or "Spirit and Word") because both are essential aspects of the work of theology and of the revelatory experience that that theology is based upon. "To affirm a theology of Word and Spirit is to affirm that the experience of faith is correlative with God's self-revelation in Jesus Christ."[27] For Bloesch, theology has "to be understood as objective-subjective rather than fundamentally objective (as in evangelical rationalism) or predominantly subjective (as in existentialism and mysticism)."[28]

4. Carl F. H. Henry, "The Priority of Divine Revelation: A Review Article," *Journal of the Evangelical Theological Society* (March 1984): 91.
5. This is the title of the first chapter of Henry's six-volume Christian apologetic (and prolegomena), *God, Revelation and Authority*, vol. 1 (Wheaton, IL: Crossway, 1999).
6. Henry, "The Priority of Divine Revelation," 92.
7. Francis Watson, *Text, Church and World: Biblical Interpretation in Theological Perspective* (Grand Rapids: Eerdmans, 1994).
8. Kevin J. Vanhoozer, *Is There a Meaning in This Text?* (Grand Rapids: Zondervan, 1998).
9. Kevin J. Vanhoozer, "God's Mighty Speech Acts," in *First Theology* (Downers Grove, IL: InterVarsity Press, 2002), 130.

10. Cf. Dulles, *Models of Revelation*, 53–66.
11. This is Dulles's point regarding Ernst Troeltsch's criticism of the supernaturalism of some forms of supernatural biblical criticism. Ibid., 53–67.
12. John Baillie, *The Idea of Revelation in Recent Thought* (New York: Columbia University Press, 1954), 50.
13. Ibid.
14. G. Ernest Wright, *God Who Acts* (London: SCM, 1966), 13.
15. Ibid., 55.
16. See Oscar Cullmann, *Salvation in History* (London: SCM, 1967), as well as Dulles, *Models of Revelation*, 56–58.
17. Alister McGrath, *The Christian Theology Reader*, 2d ed. (Oxford: Blackwell, 2001).
18. Cited in McGrath, *Reader*: Original Source is Ernst Troeltsch, "Faith and History," in *Religion in History*, trans. James Luther Adams and Walter F. Bense (Edinburgh: T & T Clark, 1991), 134–45.

19. Emil Brunner, *Truth as Encounter* (Philadelphia: Westminster, 1964), 19.
20. Ibid.
21. Ibid., 23.
22. Ibid., 28.
23. Karl Barth, *God in Action* (Manhassett, NY: Round Table, 1963), 19.
24. Donald Bloesch, *A Theology of Word and Spirit: Authority and Method in Theology* (Downers Grove, IL: InterVarsity Press, 1992), 186.

The Nature of Divine Revelation

Five Models of Revelation

Revelation as Dialectical Presence	Revelation as History	Revelation as Speech
25. Rudolf Bultmann, "The Problem of Hermeneutics," in *Essays: Philosophical and Theological* (London: SCM, 1955), 256. 26. Cf. Bloesch's *Theology of Word and Spirit*: "Dialectical theology is an open-ended theology, whose formulations are ever tentative. The synoptic vision or final synthesis belongs only to God, but we can bear witness to this through our approximate formulations" (78). 27. Ibid., 13. 28. Ibid., 14.		

The Nature of Divine Revelation

Five Models of Revelation

Revelation as Inner Experience	Revelation as New Awareness
For Friedrich Schleiermacher, the ground of the Christian, ecclesial community is the shared experience of the *feeling of absolute dependence upon God.* The idea of revelation "signifies the *originality* of the fact which lies at the foundation of a religious communion."[29] The "fact" of which he speaks is that inner experience, which is piety. Though viewing revelation as set into motion by divine governance for the purpose of furthering humanity's salvation, he was unwilling to view revelation as operating "upon man as a cognitive being . . . for that would make the revelation to be originally and essentially *doctrine*."[30] Schleiermacher does not believe that "a system of propositions," which can be understood "from their connection with others," can serve as the form and content of revelation. Such a system has no supernatural origin. Revelation, for Schleiermacher, can "only be apprehended . . . as parts of another whole, as a moment of the life of a thinking being who works upon us directly as a distinctive existence by means of his total impression upon us," which is to say upon the "self-consciousness."[31] Schleiermacher refers to various forms of mythology to suggest that numerous expressions of inspiration have occurred wherever people have generated, within themselves, a "new and peculiar idea of God," giving rise to a "distinctive worship." He concludes that any number of religious communions may have experienced and apprehended partially the truth of God through a revelation, indeed, no one religious communion can claim to have complete revelation of God, because that would mean that "God made Himself known as He is in and for Himself. . . . But such a truth could not proceed outwardly from any fact."[32] The idea of revelation, Schleiermacher asserts, "is better to apply only to the region of the higher self-consciousness."[33] Schleiermacher does posit that revelation is found in the highest, most transcendent degree in the "appearance of the Redeemer in history," in relation to which all other forms of revelation and inspiration become "nonexistence," since they are "destined to be submerged again in Him."[34] Christ alone, Schleiermacher asserts, "is destined gradually to quicken the whole human race into higher life."[35] Revelation in Christ, then, is not entirely supernatural, for all humans have the innate potential to "take up the divine into itself, just as did happen in Christ."[36] In his *Essay on Theological Method,* liberal theologian Gordon Kaufmann suggests that theology is a constructive enterprise in which the theologian uses the imagination to construct second-order, not first-order, theological concepts.[37] The theological task, he says, has a "radically constructive character" in which "imaginative construction is the proper mode—indeed the only mode—through which we can become aware of God in his full autonomy and self-integrity."[38] Theology is a "self-conscious" and "self-critical" exercise of the believer to reflect seriously on the experience of faith. For Kaufmann, knowers do not have access to a "reality" or	Revelation as new awareness, as Avery Dulles presents it, is different from others in that revelation is not something operated *upon* as a passive subject from outside. Rather, revelation "is a transcendent fulfillment of the inner drive of the human spirit toward fuller consciousness."[44] In this view, revelation is wholly a subjective experience, shedding light not on an objective object (such as God) through a mediated knowledge (such as Scripture, history, or experience) but rather on the "self and on the world as they are experienced in the whole of life."[45] Whereas Schleiermacher's view of revelation took a turn toward anthropology in its focus on inner experience, this view is completely anthropological. In it no objectively verifiable claim is made for knowledge of God or any objective metaphysical reality *through* subjectivity. Rather, God is only known through inward consciousness, a new awareness. The traditional Christian emphasis on the transcendence of God is replaced by a view of God—or of God as He makes Himself known—as utterly immanent. Dulles quotes Pierre Teilhard de Chardin saying, "God never reveals himself from outside, by intrusion, but *from within,* by stimulation and enrichment of the human psychic current, the sound of his voice being made recognizable by the fullness and coherence it contributes to our individual and collective being."[46] Dulles includes, as proponents of this view, Karl Rahner, Paul Tillich, and Langdon Gilkey. For Tillich, revelation is not a Barthian crisis event of God breaking into humanity from the outside. Rather, the ultimate questions of humanity are correlated in the event of revelation. Dulles says Gilkey "tries to show that ultimate questions are present in ordinary secular experience, and that revelation, mediated through religious symbols, meaningfully answers those questions. . . . Religious discourse, he concludes, is not, directly, talk about God but is talk about the finite with regard to its divine ground."[47] Dulles writes of H. Richard Niebuhr as an example of an innovative theologian for his work on revelation in *The Meaning of Revelation.*[48] Dulles says that Niebuhr's mediation of liberalism and Barthianism with respect to the question of revelation "in many ways foreshadowed what we have described as the 'new awareness' model."[49] We place him in this category because of his linking of personal experience (the subjective dimension) with historical account (the objective dimension) in the reception of revelation. Donald Bloesch has summarized Niebuhr's view: "Scripture without experience is empty, but experience without Scripture is blind."[50] Niebuhr noted that "there is no such thing as disinterestedness in theology."[51] Value cannot be separated from fact when it comes to the questions of meaning and religious truth with which theology deals. Theology is done within historic, religious communities that have already received a revelation. He states, "This is the sum of the matter: Christian theology must begin today with revelation because it knows that men cannot think about God save as historic, communal beings and save as believers. It must ask what revelation means for Christians rather than what it ought to mean for all men, everywhere and at all times. And it can

The Nature of Divine Revelation

Five Models of Revelation

Revelation as Inner Experience

"truth" outside of the self's capacities to realize and conceptualize through the activities of mind: "We simply do not have, and cannot even conceive what it would be like to have, any direct experience or perception of realities of this order of universality and comprehensiveness. Hence, theological issues must be adjudicated in ways other than those appropriate to the concepts of, and statements about, the objects of experience."[39]

The ability—and necessity—to so use the imagination to reflect on one's religious experience presupposes the reality of divine revelation: "it is precisely this concept, in fact, which provides the ground for claims that the alleged revelation must be regarded as authoritative." The structure of the imagination and the ability to conceptualize "God" gives the theologian "reason to regard the divine revelation as authoritative." For Kaufmann, the concept of divine revelation is necessary for "certain constructions of the concept of God, specifically those based on the model of the human person or agent."[40]

For these theological models, knowledge of God "depends upon his act of disclosure."[41] But even this does not, Kaufmann points out, invalidate the fact that theology is a construct of the imagination: "It means, rather, that it is precisely through the constructive work of the human imagination that God—ultimate reality understood as active and beneficent, as 'gracious'—makes himself known."[42] For Kaufmann the concept of God *is* revelation.[43] But the concept is derived through constructive reflection on one's religious experience.

29. Friedrich Schleiermacher, *The Christian Faith*, ed. H. R. Mackintosh and J. S. Stewart (reprint, New York: Harper & Row, 1963), 50.
30. Ibid.
31. Ibid.
32. Ibid, 52.
33. Ibid, 63.
34. Ibid, 62–63.
35. Ibid, 64.
36. Ibid.
37. Gordon Kaufmann, *An Essay on Theological Method* (Atlanta: Scholars Press, 1995).
38. Ibid, 42.
39. Ibid, 41.
40. Ibid, 81.
41. Ibid, 82.
42. Ibid.
43. Ibid.

Revelation as New Awareness

pursue its inquiry only by recalling the story of Christian life and by analyzing what Christians see from their limited point of view in history and faith."[52]

Theology is concerned with the meaning of revelation as it is received in historical, social, epistemologically limited communities. When Christians read Scripture, and thus the history it tells, they read through the eyes of faith. They *value* this history in ways that outsiders to Christianity do not. In the valuing of this story, this history, an awareness is given which would otherwise not be possible. The events of history to which Scripture refers, says Niebuhr, could be interpreted and observed from a merely objective point of view.[53] This would not be the perspective of faith; thus it would not be the reception of revelation.

The sphere in which revelation happens, Niebuhr says, is in "internal history," as distinct from "external history."[54] External history is the realm of universally observable cause and effect, of objective observation. Internal history is the realm of value, in which only members of communities who share a particular understanding and experience of faith can agree on the meanings of events—which is "memory."

Revelation, Niebuhr writes, means that part of our inner history illuminates and makes intelligible the rest of inner history. Jesus Christ makes all other events understood.[55] Revelation, then, is the illuminative event of Jesus Christ that gives meaning to existence. This meaning is the product of shared reflection on the significance of Christ within historically situated communities of believers. Revelation is not static. It "is a moving thing in so far as its meaning is realized only by being brought to bear upon the interpretation and reconstruction of ever new human situations in an enduring movement, a single drama of divine and human action. So the God who revealed himself continues to reveal himself—the one God of all times and places."[56]

44. Dulles, *Models of Revelation*, 98.
45. Ibid.
46. P. Teilhard de Chardin, *Christianity and Evolution* (New York: Harcourt Brace Jovanovich, 1971), 143, cited in Dulles, *Models of Revelation*, 99.
47. Dulles, *Models of Revelation*, 102–3.
48. H. Richard Niebuhr, *The Meaning of Revelation* (New York: Macmillan, 1941).
49. Dulles, *Models of Revelation*, 127.
50. Bloesch, *A Theology of Word and Spirit*, 189.
51. Niebuhr, *Meaning of Revelation*, 26.
52. Ibid, 31.
53. Ibid, 41.
54. Ibid, 66.
55. Ibid, 69.
56. Ibid, 99.

The Nature of Divine Revelation

General and Special Revelation: How Can God Be Known?

Revelation is God's self-disclosure to humanity for the purpose of enabling His creatures to know Him cognitively and to know Him relationally, i.e., to enjoy a covenantal relationship with Him. It could be said that Adam and Eve before the Fall did not need Scripture because they enjoyed an intimate revelation in which God communed and conversed with them in the garden. Their intimate relationship with God *was itself* a revelation, all they needed was to be in relation. After the Fall, however, humanity suffers from the results of separation from God because of sin. Yet God continues to reveal Himself, though not completely, entirely, or necessarily *as He is in Himself* to humanity. The question arises, "How does He do so?"

Theologians have sometimes divided the concept of revelation into two broad categories: natural and supernatural. God reveals Himself naturally through such vehicles as creation, human reason, intuition, and inward consciousness. God reveals Himself *supernaturally* through His spoken word, miracles, and Scripture. This distinction suffers at times from a lack of clarity and from some areas of uncertainty in delineating "supernatural" from "natural" when referring to God's self-disclosure. When referring to *any* act or revelation of God, for instance, how can one say that it is merely "natural"?

A better distinction commonly used is that of general and special revelation. God reveals Himself generally to *all* creation through creation itself, through humanity's consciousness, and through an innate moral sense. This is the message of Romans 2, that God has left His "stamp" on the universe, in the things He has made and in the people He has created. This general information, however, proves insufficient to lead people to God. Special revelation, then, is God's specific, intentional disclosure of Himself, His plan for redemption in Christ, and His will for His people, in clear, distinctive ways. This revelation is not generally accessible through general means, but is apprehended by faith in the gospel through a saving relationship with God in Christ.

Nature and grace contribute to our understanding of how revelation works. God created the world and humanity. The effects of His creation are natural. Left to their own devices, then, humans try to see in nature who they are and who God is. God also brings to bear on the world and in the minds and hearts of humans His *grace*. He does not leave them to the devices of nature only. Thus, His revelation occurs through the merits and kindnesses of His grace. His grace works in and through the elements of nature to disclose Himself, cognitively and relationally.

The significance of this discussion for theological prolegomena is clear. How do humans acquire knowledge of God (theology)? Through general revelation? Through special revelation? Through a combination of both? Does it occur by nature (i.e., is it *innate, intuitive*)? Does it happen by grace alone, through faith alone?

The Nature of Divine Revelation

How Knowledge of God Is Acquired

Natural Theology Tells Us *That God Is*, Revealed Theology Tells Us *Who God Is*	God Is Revealed Generally, but Truly Known Only Specially
Thomas Aquinas	John Calvin

Thomas Aquinas

Undoubtedly the church's greatest theologian (and certainly the most prolific) since Augustine, Thomas Aquinas (c. 1224–1274), in his *Summa Theologica*, worked often with the relationship between revelation and reason, or between natural theology and revealed theology. This is seen most explicitly in his Part 1, Question 12: "How God Is Known By Us."

How much, ponders Thomas, can the *created intellect* of humanity know about God? Can it know the divine essence? Must the divine essence be seen through a "likeness of Him"?

In order to see the likeness of God, Aquinas asserts, humanity must receive a disposition in their being (especially in their intellect) that would enable him to see and know God in His essence. He must therefore receive "the light of glory strengthening the intellect to see God."[57]

To the question, "whether any created intellect by its natural powers can see the divine essence," Thomas replies with a qualified no. By natural powers alone, the intellect cannot see God in His essence. However, because the intellect remained intact after the Fall, it is possible to see and know God when God's grace adds to and strengthens it. When "God by His grace unites Himself to the created intellect," then the creature can see God as an "object made intelligible to it."[58] A "supernatural disposition" increases the powers of the created intellect so that God can be known by it.[59] Humans cannot see God, except by what He does, just as an ultimate cause cannot be seen except in its effects. However, as the divine light illuminates the human intellect, those effects can lead to a clear knowledge of God's essence.

Can God be known by natural reason? Creatures know things naturally by their senses, he explained, and thus God can only be known by effects (which includes humans themselves) that can be seen in nature and in rational thought. Nonetheless, "Because they are His effects and depend on their cause, we can be led from them so far as to know of God *whether He exists*, and to know of Him what must necessarily belong to Him, as the first cause of all things, exceeding all things caused by Him."[60]

Through natural reason, humans can develop a limited natural theology. But this theology gives evidence of the existence of God, not necessarily *what* God is or who He is in Himself. In fact, Thomas developed his five proofs for the existence of God on the basis of natural theology. However, what is revealed by nature is of lesser perfection than that which is revealed by grace, received by faith, which itself is a kind of knowledge.

John Calvin

Calvin began his Institutes with a discussion of "the Knowledge of God the Creator," giving place at the start to a kind of general revelation. He notes that this revelation of God has been given in two ways: (1) The knowledge of God has been "naturally implanted in the minds of men" (i.e., "by natural instinct," an "awareness of divinity," and "a certain understanding of his divine majesty"), and (2) The knowledge of God "shines forth in the fashioning of the Universe and the continuing governance of it."[61]

Nonetheless, though God has stamped His imprint on man's consciousness and on creation itself, it "does not profit us," because the radical sinfulness of man's nature turns him away from God, rendering him wholly unable, in his natural state, to know God through general revelation. As he states, "The manifestation of God in nature speaks to us in vain . . ." "Although they bathe us wholly in their radiance, yet they can of themselves in no way lead us into the right path."[62]

What, then, is this general revelation good for if it does not provide actual, true knowledge of God to those who encounter it? One reason is to render humanity without excuse: "Although we lack the natural ability to mount up into the pure and clear knowledge of God, all excuse is cut off because the fault of dullness is within us."[63]

Thus special revelation, as Scripture, is needed as "Guide and Teacher" in order to know God, even as the Creator. So Calvin: "God bestows the actual knowledge of himself upon us only in the Scriptures."[64]

Thus in the Scriptures we find two kinds of the knowledge of God: God as Creator and God as Redeemer: "First in order came that kind of knowledge by which one is permitted to grasp who that God is who founded and governs the universe. Then that other inner knowledge was added, which alone quickens dead souls."[65] This latter knowledge is whereby a person comes to know God as Redeemer. The inner witness of the Spirit is necessary, given by grace through faith, to enable a person even to come to a true (and salvific) knowledge of God in the Scriptures. "Nevertheless, all things will tend to this end, that God, the Artificer of the universe, is made manifest to us in Scripture, and that what we ought to think of him is set forth there."[66]

61. John Calvin, *Institutes of the Christian Religion*, 2 vols., ed. John T. McNeill, trans. Ford Lewis Battles (Philadelphia: Westminster, 1960), 1.43, 51.

How Knowledge of God Is Acquired

Natural Theology Tells Us *That God Is*, Revealed Theology Tells Us *Who God Is*	God Is Revealed Generally, but Truly Known Only Specially
	Calvin
	62. Ibid., 68. 63. Ibid. 64. Ibid., 69. 65. Ibid., 70–71. 66. Ibid., 71.
Aquinas	
57. Thomas Aquinas, *The Summa Theologica*, in *Introduction to Thomas Aquinas*, ed. Anton C. Pegis (New York: Modern Library, 1948), 74. 58. Ibid., 78. 59. Ibid., 80. 60. Ibid., 94.	

The Nature of Divine Revelation

How Knowledge of God Is Acquired

All Theology Is Revealed Theology	Revealed Theology Finds Its "Point of Contact" in Natural Theology
Karl Barth	Emil Brunner

Karl Barth

According to the view that all theology is revealed theology, not only is salvation inaccessible to humanity apart from special revelation, but so is *any* knowledge of God.[67] This view holds that human reason, with everything else, was utterly corrupted by the fall, rendering it incapable of acquiring by its own resources *any* accurate knowledge of God and of divine things.

This view was most prominently (and vigorously) propounded by Karl Barth, who reacted against the then-common tendency to theologize on the basis of Enlightenment principles of rationality, rather than on the sole, ultimate authority of Scripture and the revelation of God in Christ.

In his "Angry Introduction" to a polemical piece against Emil Brunner's *Nature and Grace*, Barth states his view of the task of theology, in opposition to how he viewed Brunner's view of that task: "We must learn again to understand revelation as grace and grace as revelation and therefore turn away from . . . *theologia naturalis* (natural theology) by ever making new decisions and being ever controverted anew."[68] In this piece, Barth found inappropriate Brunner's "point of contact" as a description of God's revelation of Himself to humanity as created in the image of God.

For Barth, natural theology is "every (positive or negative) formulation of a system which claims to be theological, i.e., to interpret divine revelation, whose subject, however, differs fundamentally from the revelation in Jesus Christ and whose method therefore differs equally from the exposition of Holy Scripture."[69]

Barth also objects to Brunner's claim that there is in humanity a "capacity for revelation" and a "capacity (or receptivity) for words," apart from the reality of revelation. Barth means by this, of course, what is usually called *special* revelation. He asks, "What is the meaning of 'receptivity for words' if man can do nothing of himself for his salvation, if it is the Holy Spirit that gives him living knowledge of the word of the Cross?"[70]

Barth wished to maintain the freedom and sovereignty of God, along with the absolute fallenness and sinfulness of man in his understanding of the revelation of God in Christ and the corresponding possibility of man to know the Creator. He wanted to bind "nature," the things of creation, including humanity and his various possibilities, inextricably with "grace," suggesting that only in grace can humanity know anything *truly* and, of course, salvifically, about God. Thus, it made no sense for Barth to speak of a general revelation in theological language. All revelation is special, all revelation is summed up in and derived from the incarnation, cross, and resurrection of Christ.

Emil Brunner

In a famous theological dialogue, Emil Brunner countered Karl Barth's insistence that the knowledge of God *only* occurs by special revelation in the person and work of Christ. In "Nature and Grace," he posited the primacy of special revelation in Christ, while also finding room to say that general revelation provides a limited knowledge of God. For Brunner, the "creation of the world" is a "self-communication of God"; this he saw as a "fundamentally Christian" interpretation of the Scriptures.[71] Taking his departure from Romans 2, Brunner said that the "consciousness of responsibility" brings about the possibility of sin. Thus, without creation and without conscience, humanity is also without responsibility before God.

General revelation is not sufficient, however, to bring people to a saving knowledge of God. Apart from a "subjective" revelation in Christ, people will only pervert the knowledge of God in creation, such that it is limited to a pagan knowledge of "gods"—not of the true God. Only the superior revelation in Christ can open the eyes of lost humanity.

Thus, Brunner spoke of the necessity of a "double-revelation," of which the first, general revelation (such as in creation or conscience), can be truly seen and understood only by the one who has been enlightened by the second, the special revelation in Christ.[72]

For Brunner, the possibility of revelation is the possibility of "address," from God to humanity. Humans (sinful though they be, are able to receive God's special revelation, His "address," because they are created in the image of God, an image they have not completely lost because humans possesses a "capacity for words and responsibility."[73] Thus humans have the possibility to hear the Word of God, in a *formal* sense (i.e., they have ears, minds, and linguistic abilities), but they do not have the possibility to *believe* the Word of God apart from faith.[74]

It is necessary to hold tightly, although paradoxically, to the dialectic of the knowledge of one's sin and the knowledge of God. Which comes first, Brunner asks? One cannot really say, for without the knowledge of one's sin, there can be no knowledge of God (and thus grace). But without the knowledge of God, there can be no knowledge of the state of sin. This dichotomy, Brunner asserts, "is itself the essence of the state of sin."[75]

71. Brunner, *Natural Theology*, 25.
72. Ibid, 26–27.
73. Ibid, 31.

The Nature of Divine Revelation

How Knowledge of God Is Acquired

All Theology Is Revealed Theology	Revealed Theology Finds Its "Point of Contact" in Natural Theology
Barth	Brunner
	74. Ibid., 32.
	75. Ibid.
67. Cf. John Baillie's introduction to *Natural Theology: Comprising "Nature and Grace" by Professor Dr. Emil Brunner and the Reply "No!" by Dr. Karl Barth*, trans. Peter Fraenkel (London: Centary, 1946).	
68. Karl Barth's "No! Answer to Emil Brunner," in *Natural Theology*, 71.	
69. Ibid., 75.	
70. Ibid., 79.	

PART SIX

Knowledge and Language About God

Knowledge of God

In John 17:3, Jesus prays to the Father, "Now this is eternal life: that they may know you, the only true God, and Jesus Christ, whom you have sent." Theology might be described as faith and reason's seeking after the knowledge of God as He is revealed in Jesus Christ, through the Holy Spirit, in His inscripturated Word. Whether one describes the pursuit of this knowledge as a scientific, rational, experiential, devotional, or dialogical approach, the theologian should seek a transformative knowledge of the divine being, which informs one's self-understanding and one's understanding of the world.

Theologians have debated whether one can have knowledge of God (and things) in the same sense in which there can be knowledge about another person or about oneself. Or is this knowledge necessarily only analogical or distinctly limited by the knower's finitude? Can any fact be known in the complete way God knows it?

A related but more traditional debate concerns whether one can have knowledge of God as He exists in Himself (i.e., as He *knows* Himself), or whether one can only have knowledge of God as He reveals, and thus accommodates, Himself to humanity using the necessary limitations of human language in historical contexts.[1]

For our purposes it seems best to focus on the distinction between aspects of the knowledge of God using two common theological designations: (1) the conceptual or theoretical, and (2) the relational or experiential modes of knowing God.

The *conceptual* mode covers the exchange among the intellectual, rational, and revelational mediums for the purpose of acquiring a conceptual knowledge of God. This conceptual knowledge often takes an abstract or intellectualized form. Its advocates, or practitioners, seek to understand concepts, images, stories, and doctrines given in Scripture through a logical, rational deductive process or a scientific, experiential inductive process.

Much of seventeenth-century Reformed theology has been characterized by some, perhaps unfairly in cases, as focusing too squarely on the rational and conceptual knowledge of God to the exclusion of the experiential and relational. Pietistic eighteenth- and nineteenth-century theologies emerged, in part, as a reaction against a "dry" orthodoxy.

Relational, or experiential modes, emphasize a dynamic and organic process of knowing God. In this perspective, God is known less through the medium of cognition (intellect or rational understanding) than through the medium of experience. On the relational view, one knows God through encounter with Him, a process of give-and-take, in which the knowing subject can never claim to have exhaustive or definitive knowledge, because the object of knowledge is also a *subject*, who knows us better than we know Him and who continually discloses Himself in new and fresh ways.

In this view, the best way to approach the knowledge of God is through a dynamic interchange between the conceptual and the relational modes. God does make Himself understood to humans through concepts, but He also provides knowledge of Himself through experiential, relational means that go beyond what is strictly conceptual. Theology cannot be adequately defined and explained by the merely conceptual.

---

1. Cf. John Frame, *The Doctrine of the Knowledge of God* (Phillipsburg, NJ: Presbyterian & Reformed, 1987), 9–61, for a helpful discussion of these and other important debates regarding the knowledge of God.

Language About God: Religious and Theological Language

Human beings cannot escape the reality of language. We use language to communicate with each other. Most theologians believe that God uses language to communicate to us. Other than "negative" theologians who claim that God, even if He exists, cannot be the subject of meaningful definition through human language, most theologians are comfortable using human language to speak about God. For some mystical theologians, humans must use only negative language to describe reality, but they are nonetheless optimistic that some knowledge of God can result from this *via negative.*

Terrence Tilley discusses the relation between "sense" and "reference" when using religious language ("talk of God").[2] The sense of a word or sentence is its "meaning." When one uses the word *God,* one means something by the term, irrespective of whether that term or concept actually refers to anything real. The reference of a term is what the word, sentence, or concept refers to. So, when theologians discuss the referent of the concept of God, they are doing realist theology. They believe that their language actually refers to something (someone) real. Some philosophers and theologians, however, confine themselves to discussions of "sense" when using religious language and talking of God. They prefer to think of the theological task as that of giving subjective meaning to human existence or subscribing a way to live, irrespective of whether their theological language actually refers meaningfully to an existing God. So Tilley says the adult who speaks about Santa Claus is speaking with a "sense," a meaning, but which has no "reference" in the real world.

For theologians who do subscribe to a realist view of religious and theological language, it is difficult to imagine the possibility of *knowing* God apart from His gift to us of language. God has always revealed Himself in direct relationship with humans through language. In the beginning God *spoke* to Adam and Eve in the Garden of Eden. However literally one takes the account, and however akin to audible human speech one imagines God's voice to be in such a setting, the inscripturated account of God's actions in history depict God using language to communicate knowledge of Himself to human creatures. And the means of communicating these descriptions in the text of Scripture is with written language (originally Hebrew, Aramaic, and Greek).

It behooves us to consider how we might express *through* language the knowledge of God that we *receive* through language. We need to ask *how* language communicates the truth and knowledge of God and to what extent human language is limited in its capacity to express theological truth. The objectives of theology differ, depending on a particular theologian's view of the capacity of language (both divine revelation and human reflection on that revelation) to refer meaningfully to God and ultimate reality. Three perspectives have typically governed these discussions: Communication is (1) univocal, (2) equivocal, or (3) analogical.

---

2. Terrance Tilley, *Talking of God: An Introduction to Philosophical Analysis of Religious Language* (New York: Paulist, 1978), 2.

Language About God

Some hold that the words we use about God represent the divine being exactly or at least adequately. The "meaning" of a word, sentence, or utterance is the same whether it is applied to finite reality or to God. Thus, "God is good" means essentially the same thing as "John is good." God's goodness will exceed in perfection John's goodness, but it will not be essentially different. This is a "univocal" view of theological language. Language is *unified* with the reality it represents, depicts, or symbolizes. Theologians who ascribe to a univocal view typically turn to a doctrine of propositional revelation and assert an optimistic view of humanity's ability to understand that revelation. God tells about Himself and reality in Scripture through propositions, truths, that can be understood with sufficient clarity by recipients of that revelation. Theology, in this view, is often seen as the task of examining the Bible's content for propositional truth.

For some theologians who subscribe to a univocal view of religious language, when we speak truly about reality, we speak in a way that equals God's knowledge (and language use) as regards that item of knowledge. "Univocal" means that a word is used, and understood, the same way in two different settings or contexts. To say our language is univocal with God's is to say that we mean the same thing God "means" by a concept or term that we use of Him or of reality. Our language, and the reality to which that language really refers, as well as God's understanding of that reality, are one and the same (although some might speak in terms of "degrees" of difference or understanding or of knowledge).

Gordon Clark, in his debate with Cornelius Van Til, argued the possibility of univocity in our use of theological language. He wished to avoid the kind of skepticism to which one might be prone if one held to an equivocal view, or even extreme analogical view, of theological language, under which the terms, concepts, and images we employ when speaking about God do not equal God's own understanding of the referents of that language. Thus, for Clark, when we say "2 + 2 = 4," we are saying (and knowing) exactly as if God says and knows it. Similarly when we say "God is holy," and we then say "St. Augustine was holy," we mean by "holy" the same thing. The only difference is in the degree of holiness (God's holiness is perfect, our temporal holiness is only derivative and imperfect), not the quality of the characteristic. Thus, for Clark, holiness is holiness, whether spoken of in reference to God or to humans. It differs in degree, not in kind. We know exactly what we mean when we say "holy," and we mean by "holy" *essentially* what God means by "holy."[3]

In his book, *Language and Theology*, Clark considers a number of modern and contemporary views of the philosophy of language and the theology of language. Clark argues that in the Bible, "the rational God gives man an intelligible message."[4] God uses words, which are symbols or signs, to disclose truth to man. For Clark, words enable men to receive and describe thoughts, thus arriving at true knowledge of God and reality: "The Christian view . . . is that God created Adam as a rational mind. The structure of Adam's mind was the same as God's. . . . This Christian view of God, man, and language does not fit into any empirical philosophy. It is rather a type of *a priori* rationalism."[5] Through propositional revelation, God gives humanity universal truths, access to which can only be through logic and reason. Also a propositionalist with respect to revelation, Carl F. H. Henry was disenchanted with Aquinas's attempt to steer a middle road between univocity and equivocacy in religious/theological language. Eliminating univocity in religious language, Henry believed, leads inevitably to skepticism. He states: "The logical difficulty with the theory of analogical predication lies in its futile attempt to explore a middle road between univocity and equivocacy. Only univocal assertions protect us from equivocacy; only univocal knowledge is, therefore, genuine and authentic knowledge. . . . Unless we have some literal truth about God, no similarity between man and God can in fact be predicated."[6]

For Henry, and others who share his position, a univocity in human, theological language about God is available because God has revealed Himself in human (and propositional) language through the writings of Scripture. Thus we can trust in the depictions of Scripture to ascribe and describe the being of God and His relation to the world in fully adequate terms, and in terms that would represent God as He actually is and as He understands things to be.

1. Human Language Is Meaningfully Descriptive of Divine Reality: Univocal

Knowledge and Language About God

Charts *on* Prolegomena

Language About God

2. Language Is Not Meaningfully Descriptive of Ultimate Reality: Equivocal

Some theologians hold that the religious language we use has no essential point of contact with God's language or His knowledge. This equivocal view holds that the same word or proposition used to describe something or someone in finite reality cannot mean the same thing when applied to God's existence. Our language fails to meaningfully describe ultimate reality, especially the reality of God. We must make an attempt through language to speak of the world we cannot see—we are obligated by our entrapment in language itself—but we should understand that all theological language is an equivocation with God's language, and with the reality to which our language attempts to refer. The underlying assumption is that God is beyond all human cognition, and language serves as a "negative way" to arrive at some kind of true sense of ultimate reality. Dan Stiver sums up this position thusly: "This tradition sees language as valuable only in the sense of being evocative of an experience of the divine or the ultimate."[7]

In the eighteenth century, theologians had to respond to the criticisms of David Hume and A. J. Ayer regarding what they saw as the senselessness of talk about God. Hume was an empiricist who believed that the only meaningful language humans can use is that which can be verified by "experimental reasoning."[8] Ayer, known for his association with the philosophical school called "logical positivism," subscribed to the "verification principle," which held that all language is meaningless unless it can be verified as being analytic and tautological (a statement whose truth is self-evident by the nature of the syntax: for example, "all bachelors are unmarried men") or proven by empirical observation or scientific method.[9] Ayer viewed religious and theological statements as necessarily meaningless because they could neither be verified nor falsified. This position did not hold currency for long. Besides the obvious devaluation of so much of the human experience of the divine, of the mystical, and other empirically unverifiable realities, the position could not even hold up to its own scrutiny, for the verification principle could not itself be verified.[10]

Theologians who subscribe to a form of equivocal language do not accept the skeptical conclusions of Ayer and Hume. For some who hold to this perspective of theological language, the most that language can do is to speak negatively of ultimate reality, thus shedding light, perhaps, on what it is by stating what it is not. By stating what *is* the case, while recognizing that one can never truly state what *is*, then one assumes that by the statement something has been brought into the light. Some have referred to this kind of theologizing as "negative theology," or "radical theology." In extreme forms, the assumption is given that one cannot even speak of God's existence, much less say anything meaningfully about Him.

Theologians who hold firmly to the necessity of equivocation in human language about the being and nature of God typically posit something like an "infinite qualitative distinction" between God and humanity, to the conclusion that all talk about God fails to refer adequately to reality. Terrence Tilley points out that this does not mean that the "sense" of religious language is meaningless, but that any talk of *reference* is. Vincent Brümmer uses this term to categorize those theologians who think of religious/theological language as being equivocal in this way. He suggests that for them the semantic difference between speaking of humanity and speaking of God is so great that one can only speak paradoxically or dialectically when attempting to refer to God. For some, any kind of real "reference" to God is impossible via language, though for others, while human language is severely limited in describing God's existence and nature, it can surely "refer" in some real way to a reality beyond our understanding, i.e., God.[11]

While one might think that this perspective necessarily eschews any talk about God revealing Himself to humanity, this is not necessarily the case. We might be able to, as Brümmer notes, experience God as He has revealed Himself to us, but not experience Him as He really is in Himself. This latter view comes closer to a kind of view of analogous language, and in some cases would be, but to the extent that some hold that human concepts, even though given through revelation, are entirely unable to arrive at a true knowledge of God's being at any meaningful *cognitive* level, and should be spoken of in the terms of equivocation.

Don Cupitt is a contemporary example of a theologian who accepts the equivocal nature of religious language but who yet attempts to provide religious meaning through theological reflection, even while accepting the limitations of theology to refer to metaphysical reality.

70

Language About God

The analogical approach attempts to steer *via media* between the univocal and the equivocal understandings of religious language. In this view, words, sentences, and concepts have similar meanings when applied to the infinite, e.g., God. However, the similarity is by way of analogy rather than by way of equality. Thus, God's love is *like* the love that a father or mother has for a child, but it is so different that, though we can posit analogy, we cannot posit *equality* between the two concepts.

Thomas Aquinas, wanting to elucidate a mediating position between the univocal and equivocal perspectives of theological language, said that God can be spoken of, and thus in some sense known, through an "analogy of being." For Aquinas, humans can come to say certain things about God, and understand what is meant by those statements and concepts, by thinking of what those same words and concepts mean when applied to the natural world (humans, animals, and things). This concept of theological language worked directly in tandem, for Aquinas, with his fairly high estimate of the ability of humans to learn things about ultimate reality, the existence of God, and God's nature (though not his complete, essential nature) through natural revelation.

For Aquinas, language about God is typically neither univocal nor completely equivocal. If language were equivocal, then His revelation, both general and special (nature and Scripture), would be essentially meaningless. However, if it were univocal, then God's being would be no longer be separated in any essential way from humanity's being and knowledge of Him. He states, "When the word 'wise' is used in relation to a human being, it so to speak delimits and embraces the aspect of humanity that it signifies. This, however, is not the case when it is used of God: what it signifies in God is not limited by our meaning of the word, but goes beyond it. Hence it is clear that the word 'wise' is not used in the same sense of God and a human being, and the same is true of all other words, so they cannot be used univocally of God and creatures."[12]

Aquinas discussed two primary aspects of analogy: The first is the analogy of attribution, in which concepts are taken from one sphere of life and *attributed* to another. When the Bible tells us that God is a "rock," we *attribute* to God the qualities we associate with rock (firm foundation, solid, dependable, etc.) even though we know that the "rock" image is only metaphorical.

The analogy of proportion is similar to the analogy of attribution, but it focuses on a similarity of concepts when used in two spheres, with the difference being only one of proportion (lesser or greater). Because God is the source of all being, every characteristic of every thing can be said to be imperfect reflections of the perfect characteristics represented only in God as Creator of all things. We might say that Socrates, for example, is wise. Socrates' wisdom can be spoken of *proportionally* and in relation to the wisdom that is possessed by and expressed in human life. By analogy, then, we can understand God's wisdom in light of what it means for Socrates to be wise. But we must take care to understand God's wisdom in *proportion* to His divine nature and the perfections He possesses. Thus, God's wisdom can be understood only in part through our understanding of Socrates' wisdom. For God's wisdom is perfect and divine and thus outside of our ability to fully comprehend it.

As Aquinas says in speaking of words such as "good" and "wise," in relation to God, "From the point of view of what the word means it is used primarily of God and derivatively of creatures, for what the word means—the perfection it signifies—flows from God to the creature. But from the point of view of our use of the word we apply it first to creatures because we know them first."[13]

Barth rejects univocity because it undermines the hiddenness of God and he rejects equivocity because it undermines the revealedness of God. This double-rejection leads Barth to the view of the "analogy of faith" (*analogia fidei*) in slight distinction from Aquinas's "analogy of being" (*analogia entis*). The analogy of faith provides us with a way of speaking about and knowing God through language and the dialectical, dialogical encounter with the Word. It is only through God's revelation that is received by faith that He speaks to humans through His Word in freedom by which we can know anything at all about Him. This is, of course, corollary to Barth's position that there is no such thing as natural theology.

As Brümmer points out, however, "Barth rejects the *analogia entis* [analogy of being] only as a basis for natural knowledge of God but does not reject the analogy between God and us as a basis for our talk about God."[14] The theologian must take care to limit talk of God to that which is received and understood through the revelatory encounter, keeping the hiddenness and the revealedness of God in dialectical tension.

3. Our Language Refers to God's Reality Indirectly but Meaningfully: Analogical

71

Language About God

3. Cf. Frame, *Doctrine of the Knowledge of God*, 21ff.
4. Gordon Clark, *Language and Theology* (Jefferson, MD: Trinity Foundation, 1980), 138.
5. Ibid., 139.
6. Carl F. H. Henry, *God, Revelation, and Authority* (reprint, Wheaton, IL: Crossway, 1999), 2:364.
7. Dan Stiver, *The Philosophy of Religious Language* (Oxford: Blackwell, 1994), 16.
8. Tilley, *Talking of God*, 5.
9. Ibid., 9.
10. Henry, *God, Revelation, and Authority*, 2:347ff.
11. Vincent Brümmer, *Speaking of a Personal God: An Essay in Philosophical Theology* (New York: Cambridge University Press, 1992), 37–40.
12. Thomas Aquinas, *Summa Theologiae*, Ia q.13, aa. 5–6, cited in Alister McGrath, *The Christian Theology Reader* (Oxford: Blackwell, 1995), 20.
13. Thomas Aquinas, *Summa Theologiae*, cited in McGrath, *The Christian Theology Reader*, 21.
14. Brümmer, *Speaking of a Personal God*, 47.

PART SEVEN
Hermeneutics and Theological Interpretation

Introductory Issues

Hermeneutics is often defined as "the science and art of interpretation." The interpreter seeks to understand and to explain the meaning of a text, whether in written, verbal, or visual form. The purpose is to communicate that meaning to others or simply to appropriate the meaning personally. Hermeneutics became a more clearly defined *theoretical* enterprise with the advent of Romantic hermeneutics (e.g., Friedrich Schleiermacher or Wilhelm Dilthey), but the practices and principles of interpretation have been discussed, analyzed, and of course used since the beginning of time (recall Satan "interpreting" God's words to Adam and Eve). In theology, well-known "hermeneuts" have represented all kinds of theological perspectives and periods. Christianity has often been called a religion "of the book," and thus it makes sense that hermeneutics would take up a good deal of space and energy in the work of theology. Some have even suggested that theology is no more nor less than the practice of hermeneutics on theologically oriented and sacred texts. While this may be overstating the case, it is certainly true that theology is hermeneutical. To neglect this fact is to neglect our historical and finite situation, even though we have a divinely given revelation.

In theology, hermeneutics has often been divided into two primary arenas: *general hermeneutics* and *special hermeneutics*.

General hermeneutics operates under the assumption that texts can and should be interpreted using universally valid methods and procedures for deriving the meaning of a text and its application. This perspective often takes on a kind of "methodological atheism," in which the methods of interpretation are available to anyone who chooses to use them, regardless of their convictions and presuppositions. So long as the correct interpretive methods are applied rightly to a text (and the methods depend on the type of text one is interpreting), an adequate understanding will emerge. Whether the interpreter is a Christian, and whether the text is the Bible, the same methods will be employed in interpreting it. This does not mean that the interpreter cannot have a presupposition that the Bible is, for example, the divinely inspired Word of God. But the presupposition does not affect the way of approaching the interpretation. Literary interpretation, for example, would interpret a Shakespearean sonnet in the same way and with the same kinds of sensitivities to language and genre as one would bring to a Davidic psalm. The difference would be in the content of the interpretation, not the method of arriving at it.

Special hermeneutics approaches the interpretation of certain texts differently than it does other texts. This is not simply a matter of genre, for general hermeneutics also makes a distinction between the way in which one would approach different genres. Rather, special hermeneutics holds that the uniqueness of a certain text, such as the Bible, demands that a different set of criteria, questions, and methods be employed in the interpretation of it. The presuppositions that underlie the Christian view of the Bible, such as human sinfulness, noetic fallibility, and divine inspiration and inerrancy, imply that the Bible must be read and interpreted with procedures one would not employ when interpreting another literary text. Thus, one might suggest, as has often been done in the history of the church, that there is more than one "level" of understanding when reading a biblical text. There is a normal, plain level of understanding (the historical/grammatical level) and there is a higher, spiritual plane of understanding that is only granted to the reader who has faith and is enlightened by the Spirit of God. Special hermeneutics, then, would commend an intense attention not only to the historical-grammatical-literary levels of the text, but also to the spiritual and existential levels of understanding and appropriation of the text in question. This assumption, by those who have held it, has often led hermeneuts to speak of the requirement of biblical interpreters: that not only should they be astute readers (or at least adequate readers/hearers) but that they also be regenerated by the Spirit and attentive to the Spirit's work in their lives as He guides them into the truth of His Word.

Hermeneutics and Theological Interpretation

Another important distinction when discussing hermeneutics is the question of determinate or indeterminate meaning in interpretation. Can the meaning or point of a text be determined with validity according to public criteria, or are the meanings of texts indeterminate, endlessly open with no way of discerning better or worse, faithful or unfaithful, adequate or inadequate interpretations? Some postmodern interpreters who adhere to and practice a *hermeneutic of suspicion* hold that the meaning of any text is indeterminate. Some who hold to indeterminacy prefer to drop the term *meaning* altogether. On this view one cannot determine, using publicly accessible criterion and/or procedures of interpretation, what the meaning, or meanings, of a text actually is. This is because there is no such thing as a meaning or meanings embedded in the text itself, just waiting to be discovered by the application of adequate methods and procedures. The reader is left to subjectivity to create meaning by reading, hearing, or viewing the text. In this view, the author is dead and has no inherent authority or measure of control in the interpretive process. The reader is not concerned with what the author may or may not have intended in the act of writing or communicating.

Others hold that the meaning of a text is determinate. That is, the interpreter has adequate access to the meaning or meanings of a text by employing appropriate interpretive procedures. The genre and style determine the kind of interpretive approach. By interpreting the text adequately, the text can be understood, exegeted, translated, or explained. One can *determine,* with some measure of adequacy and according to some measure of publicly accessible criteria, what the meaning or meanings of a text actually are. On this view, it is possible for one's interpretation to be critiqued by another interpreter, according to generally accepted norms and criteria of what makes for an adequate interpretation of a text.

The task of theology cannot avoid the process of hermeneutics—of understanding texts by interpreting them. Some theologies are more consciously hermeneutical than others. These take into account linguistic and cultural differences between the biblical writers and the contemporary reader. They consider the interpretive difficulties that these differences bring about. Other theologies are not so forthright about the hermeneutical issues involved, and assume that by employing proper interpretive methods the correct and final meaning can be adequately, clearly, and perhaps even finally, understood in the text.

Hermeneutics and Theological Interpretation

Charts on Prolegomena

Types of Hermeneutics

In this section, various types of, and approaches to, hermeneutics are organized around the subjective/objective distinction that was used to locate various approaches to theology in general. This is appropriate because hermeneutics lies within the theological task and reflects a theological method. As goes hermeneutics (the approach to and practice of interpretation), so goes theology. To quickly get a grasp on where various hermeneutical positions lie in relation to the objective/subjective distinction, we will discern where each position places the locus of "meaning." Does meaning reside in the text itself, regardless of the role of an interpreter? Does meaning reside in the interpreter alone, as he or she brings meaning to the text? Or does meaning reside in the interaction, the combination of the two, or in something else altogether?

We must also note whether meaning is single or multiple in each approach. Does each text have a single, fixed meaning or multiple and variant meanings? Can a text be given a fuller meaning (*sensus plenior*) than what was originally intended by the first author and originally understood by the initial recipients?

Finally, when doing theology, what kind of hermeneutical approach should be taken? Should theology be tied to an objective hermeneutic or a subjective hermeneutic?

Objective Hermeneutics

1. Benjamin Jowett and the Determinacy of the Text

Benjamin Jowett wrote an essay in which he defended the view that each text has a single meaning. He was concerned that some pastors tend to "exaggerate or amplify the meaning of simple words for the sake of edification."[1] In this process they do not preserve the true meaning. Though the interpreter should have a religious and theological interest in reading Scripture, as opposed to reading other texts, the Bible should be interpreted just like any other book. Thus, what is needed for interpretation of Scripture is not a special hermeneutic but a general hermeneutic—one that applies to any text. While the subject matter of the Bible is different from that of other books, Jowett said that difference will not alter the interpreter's methods.

Jowett argued for a "general hermeneutic," in which, regarding "the meaning of words, the connection of sentences, the settlement of the text, the evidence of facts, the same rules apply to the Old and New Testaments as to any other books."[2] In a statement starkly at odds with the "new hermeneutic" idea that all interpretation is conditioned by the historical situation of the *reader*, not the author, Jowett says, "The office of the interpreter is not to add another [meaning], but to recover the original one; the meaning, that is of the words as they struck on the ears or flashed before the eyes of those who first heard and read them. He has to transfer himself to another age; to imagine that he is a disciple of Christ or Paul; to disengage himself from all that follows."[3] Jowett goes on to say that the ideal interpreter of the Bible would distance himself from the doctrines espoused throughout church history and all propounded theories of interpretation: "He has no theory of interpretation; a few rules guarding against common errors are enough for him. His object is to read Scripture like any other book, with a real interest and not merely a conventional one. He wants to be able to open his eyes and see or imagine things as they really are."[4]

While many theologians appreciate Jowett's emphasis on returning to the text as it is and interpreting it objectively, this view is seen by many as naïve or even unchristian. It has become commonplace knowledge that readers cannot escape presuppositions and biases when they come to the text. Because the distance of time and worldview between the biblical writers and its contemporary readers cannot finally be displaced, Jowett's ideal seems naïve to some. Jowett also would have readers neglect the theological insights and developments of the history of the Christian church, with its creeds and confessions. Many theologians would view this as a non-Christian idea that would impoverish the task of interpretation, not enrich it.

77

Hermeneutics and Theological Interpretation

Types of Hermeneutics

2. E. D. Hirsch: Right Interpretations Are Determined by Author's Meaning	E. D. Hirsch has made an indelible impression upon hermeneutical theory in the humanities. His defense of the importance of authorial intention and of the objectivity of textual interpretation has influenced theological hermeneutics. In the wake of Rudolf Bultmann's existential, subjective biblical hermeneutics and the turn away from authorial intention in Hans-Georg Gadamer's significant work, *Truth and Method*, Hirsch expounded what he saw as the crucial distinction between meaning and significance in the interpretation of texts.

For Hirsch, the meaning the author intended is the only truly normative and universally compelling standard for determining a text's meaning: "On purely practical grounds, therefore, it is preferable to agree that the meaning of a text is the author's meaning."[5]

In contrast to the "new hermeneutic" of his day, which shifted the emphasis in determining textual meaning from the author's intent and/or the original recipients' likely understanding of a text, Hirsch held that textual meanings do not change according to the reader and the time in which a text is read. "As soon as the reader's outlook is permitted to determine what a text means, we have not simply a changing meaning but quite possibly as many meanings as readers."[6]

If meaning changes with time and with readers, then the foundation and objectivity of textual meaning is lost. There can be no *validity in interpretation*, no agreement between readers or criterion for determining better or worse interpretations of texts if the author's intention is not the basis for determining meaning.[7]

Hirsch points out, however, that textual meaning should not always be equated with an author's "psychic" acts, because there may be instances where "inexplicit" or "unsaid" implications may be derived from a text by the interpreter that were not necessarily conscious, psychic acts of the author.

Hirsch is perhaps best known for positing a clear delineation between the meaning and the significance(s) of a text. The meaning does not change. It is fixed by the act of writing and must be determined in reference to the author's intentional action. The significance of a text for the reader does change, depending on the reader's current understanding and situation that he or she brings to the text. So Hirsch:

"There is a difference between the meaning of a text (which does not change) and the meaning of a text to us today (which changes). The meaning of a text is that which the author meant by his use of particular linguistic symbols. Being linguistic, this meaning is communal, that is, self-identical and reproducible in more than one consciousness. Being reproducible, it is the same whenever and wherever it is understood by another. However, each time this meaning is construed, its meaning to the construer (its significance) is different. Since his situation is different, so is the character of his relationship to the construed meaning. It is precisely because the meaning of the text is always the same that its relationship to a different situation is a different relationship."[8] |
| **3. James Barr: Meaning of the Bible Is Its Historical Production and Present Use** | James Barr, in an essay titled "The Bible as a Document of Believing Communities," points to the dynamic, personal, and historical nature of the formulation of the biblical text (and canon). For Barr, it is a mistake to seek to determine the meaning of the Bible only in reference to the written biblical text while neglecting the communal and historical nature of the text's origin. What was written in the Old Testament was the histories (and memories) of the people of God as they experienced God throughout a very long period of time. The New Testament Gospels were written down, but only after the gospel story of Jesus became an oral tradition. This oral tradition, for Barr, comprised and presented the "essential word of life in New Testament Christianity."[9]

Today, the Bible gives its readers (members of individual Christian or Jewish faith communities) the "classic literary expression of the people of God's experience in their contact with God. Interlaced as the whole is with theology, theology or doctrine is not the prime form in which it speaks. It speaks rather in the voice of a people's hymns in praise of its God, in the moral instructions and counsels of its teachers, in the utterances of prophets for such or such a time, in letters and occasional papers, but most of all, of course, in narrative."[10]

Barr appreciates the diverse collection of literary forms in Scripture, as well as the diverse landscape of historical representation. He sees its diversity to be the center of its power as a classic religious expression in providing religious communities a basis for prayer, worship, liturgy, |

Types of Hermeneutics

etc. The Bible, as the source of contemporary Christian life and worship, must be interpreted adequately for its meaning. He states that a genuine attempt must be "made to discover and interpret what it really means, as against our antecedent expectation of what it ought to mean." In order to interpret the Bible properly for its meaning (and thus to provide a structure for Christians to live out its basic paradigms), the disciplines outside of biblical and theological fields should be employed: "only that can guard us from systematic misunderstanding of the range of possible meanings of biblical terms in their reference to present and future." Thus, while Barr focuses the task of interpretation (and so hermeneutics) on the meaning of the text as it has come to the religious community, that meaning can neither be fully understood without reference to its dynamic and historical production by and within a community of faith (Israel, the early church, etc.) as well as with reference to its appropriation by very different, historically speaking, subsequent communities of reception. For Barr, the meaning of the Bible lies in its historical production as well as its present use. But its present meaning awaits an adequate interpretation that employs proper hermeneutical methods with a strong degree of objectivity.

4. Francis Watson: Biblical Text as Communicative Action

Francis Watson, in *Text and Truth*,[11] replies to a prevalent postmodern perspective that views texts as indeterminate. He says that the *fact* of a multiplicity of interpretations of a single text does not argue for the necessity of indeterminacy with respect to interpretation. Rather, the reality of varying interpretations of a text can be traced to misinterpretations and "varying interpretive paradigms."[12] These alternative explanations are "compatible with the view that a text has or may have a single, literal sense, a thread to guide one through the labyrinthine complexities of interpretation."[13]

Noting the difficulties of retaining the concept of a "single sense," Watson contends that it "is valuable in preserving the insight that the text as a communicative act ultimately intends one thing and not another. Any act of communication is directed towards a particular addressee, upon whom it intends a particular effect; and this directedness is inherent in the communication itself."[14]

Watson discusses the work of Frank Kermode, *The Classic*, and *The Genesis of Secrecy*, who argues that the Bible's status as "classic" text means that in any single biblical text there exists a "plurality of significances."[15] The biblical text is indeterminate, Kermode argues, offering to its readers a limitless play of pleasure in interpretation (a "thoroughgoing relativism"), which fits perfectly within the pluralistic discourse of postmodernism. Kermode interprets the gospel of Mark as essentially an indeterminate and interpretively obscure text that serves only to show the reader that he or she is always an "outsider" to its meaning (or meaninglessness). Watson says that Kermode misses the point of the existence of the biblical texts. They are results of intentional communicative action, meant to communicate good news. The gospel is good news, Watson says, light shining in a dark place—darkness obscuring light. If Mark is *gospel*, Watson says, it "cannot be multiple or opaque."[16]

Watson points to three elements of a postmodern paradigm for biblical interpretation: (1) The "dogma of the single sense" of biblical texts must be abandoned: "No text has a single meaning, fixed for all time."[17] (2) "Meaning is determined not by authors but by readers. . . . Interpretation is therefore necessarily pluralistic."[18] (3) The resulting plurality of interpretations, including explicitly religious or theological interpretations, should be seen as an advantage, not a disadvantage. Theological readings are thus given equal treatment in the marketplace of interpretive possibilities. This is good for theology. But as Watson points out, this situation really leads only to pluralism, not to a positive stake for theological witness to the reality of Christ.

The three elements listed above of this postmodern paradigm must be rejected, Watson asserts, "because they conflict with the dogmas held to be foundational to orthodox Christian faith, and because, in the light of that conflict, certain inherent problems and implausibilities rapidly come to light. . . . A Christian faith concerned to retain its own coherence cannot for a moment accept that the biblical texts (individually and as a whole) lack a single, determinate meaning, that their meanings are created by their readers, or that theological interpretations must see themselves as non-privileged participants in an open-ended, pluralistic conversation."[19] The Bible-as-classic view, within the postmodern

Types of Hermeneutics

paradigm, cannot sustain a coherent Christian witness as Christian Scripture: a "witness to the decisive series of events which God is held to have uniquely disclosed himself, and to the pattern of life shaped in response to that self-disclosure."[20]

In order to account for the status and content of Scripture as an authoritatively unique *witness* to God's redemptive and revelatory acts, Watson commends a robust view of communicative action and a return to some "unfashionable concepts" (e.g., determinate meaning, objective interpretation, and authorial intention as a way of determining the boundaries of the text's possible meaning).

5. Kevin Vanhoozer: The Meaning in the Text Is a Result of Canonical Communication

Kevin Vanhoozer wrote a significant book, *Is There a Meaning in This Text?* to answer a rising tide of unbelief in some postmodern circles of deconstruction literary theory regarding the possibility of determining meaning in a text. The "masters of suspicion" operate under the assumption that the "author is dead," so authorial intent has little to no objective control over the discernment and appropriation of meaning in the texts. For the deconstructionists, readers are free to create their own meanings. Deconstructionists argue that other interpreters have succumbed to the authority of texts and to authors and contributed to the perpetuation of idol worship: They have bowed down to authoritarian metanarratives. Vanhoozer asks, Is it idolatrous to believe in a single correct interpretation? Is it possible that, in the name of interpretation, some might seek to control God Himself, or at least God's *Word*? "Is there not a real danger of mistaking one's interpretation, which is always secondary, contextual, and never ultimate, for the text itself—a danger we might call the *idolatry of literary knowledge?* If so, then it is important to add that *what is idolatrous is not the belief in a single correct interpretation but rather the conviction that it is our exclusive possession.*"[21]

We can take seriously the deconstructionist warning that obsession with finding a single meaning *in* a text can lead to idolatry. But placing the authority of one's own interpretation over the Bible itself misuses and abuses power through interpretative actions. Vanhoozer holds that an "ethics of interpretation" must serve as "an alternative between the absolutely knowable and the absolutely undecidable." This alternative, Vanhoozer claims, begins with "a proper fear of the other, of the author."[22]

Vanhoozer's proposal draws on the Hirsch distinction between *meaning* and *significance,*[23] giving meaning the metaphysical pride of place, for meaning comes from the communicative act of the author. Significance is the way in which the text's meaning bears on the reader. Significance is how meaning applies to the reader's own life, becoming existentially relevant in a particular way.

For Vanhoozer, the Bible is the canonical, divine speech act through which the Trinitarian God spoke first through the prophets and other biblical writers and second to His people in every subsequent generation. This emphasis on the canonical speech act of God allows for a richer meaning of Scripture, associated with divine authorship[24] because it takes into account the varieties of genres, languages, and semantic fields through which God has spoken. This emphasis also lets the parts be interpreted by the whole, and the whole by the parts.

Types of Hermeneutics

6. Historical-Critical Interpretation: The Meaning Is the True Historical Account Represented by the Text

Historical-critical interpretation arose as a dominant form of biblical interpretation in the pre-Enlightenment period and reached its zenith in the theological institutions of Germany in the late nineteenth century. The intent of most of its proponents was to study and analyze the biblical text as a literary and historical document, rather than as a sacred, theological, and spiritual authoritative text. These scholars figured that study of the biblical text's spiritual implications might be a valid way to approach the Bible in other arenas, but not in academic study. Thus, the intention of historical criticism was to be objective. This intention of objectivity has not held true, however.[25] Further, the contemporary emphasis on the inescapability of presuppositions (philosophical, religious, and ideological) has demonstrated that historical criticism also succumbs to subjective interpretative interests.

Historical criticism has taken many forms over the years of its dominance in the realm of academic biblical studies. The four major approaches to historical criticism are *form criticism*, *source criticism*, *tradition criticism*, and *redaction criticism*. All these approaches to criticism focus on the literature and history of the biblical text and use "objective" methods of interpretation and criticism that could be applied generally to the study of any ancient text. Thus it is more a general hermeneutic than a special hermeneutic. Form criticism examines particular texts according to their classification as literary types, such as parables, sayings, and wisdom literature. Source criticism examines the history behind the text in terms of composition: Who were the author or authors? Who were the editor or editors? Tradition criticism examines the way in which various narratives, histories, and myths (traditions) were appropriated and expounded upon by the biblical authors or editors.[26] Redaction criticism discusses the theological points of view of the biblical authors as can be discerned indirectly, through the content and style of their writings. Friedrich Schleiermacher's (father of modern liberalism) divinatory hermeneutics hold that the primary concern and goal of the reader is to discern and empathize with the original author's psychological intentions. The intentions are, of course, "behind" the text as it stands. Critics have moved beyond Schleiermacher's lofty and unattainable goal, since we have no access to a long-dead author's psyche and since we often, thanks to source, form, and redaction criticism, have no satisfactory knowledge of *who* the author or authors really were.

Modern historical criticism (or "higher criticism") seeks a reconstruction of the source and origins of ancient texts, or information on a text through a comparison of the form of a text with forms of other relevant texts of a specific period or genre. Oftentimes historical criticism employs its methods to determine what in the biblical text is considered authentic. What words and actions of Jesus really are historical truth and what is simply redacted into the text by writers of the church.

Modern liberal historical critics often do not seek a religious meaning (certainly not a normative, transcendent religious meaning) in the text. Rather, they read *into* or *through* a text's plain sense and structure to discern (if possible) the history *behind* a text. Old Testament texts, then (for example, God's mighty acts for His people Israel as they crossed from Egypt into the Promised Land), are read for the kernel of historical information we can discern through the mythical stories and embellishments about a curious, ancient people group called the Israelites. Given a modern, scientific worldview, these critics presuppose that the miraculous accounts depicted by these ancient peoples could not possibly be true in the way they are depicted. The supposition is that enough evidence exists to make study profitable to learn what we can about the real history of the people behind the stories by "demythologizing" them.

Hermeneutics and Theological Interpretation

Types of Hermeneutics

Subjective Hermeneutics

7. Donald Bloesch: Historical-Pneumatic Hermeneutics

Donald Bloesch delineates a variety of contemporary options for theological hermeneutics.[27] For his own part, he suggests as the most appropriate model a "historical-pneumatic hermeneutics," in which "Word and Spirit are joined together in dynamic unity."[28] In this hermeneutical approach, one views the text as a "prism, through which the light of God shines on us. It is not itself the light, but it relays the light to us."

Bloesch often states his appreciation for Karl Barth's theological insights, though Bloesch himself attempts to construct a doctrine of the Word of God and a theological hermeneutic more in accord with the Reformers' emphasis on the inspiration of revelation. Bloesch is reluctant to speak of meaning as ontologically (and exclusively) residing in the biblical text itself. That would be to fall prey, Bloesch suggests, to the errors of biblical fundamentalism. Rather, for Bloesch, "The meaning of the text is located in the mind of the divine author of Scripture, and not until this author speaks can we know the full implications of the text before us."[29]

The Word of God, Bloesch says, is tied to the Bible, but it is also broader than the Bible. This is the only way to affirm, Bloesch contends, both the divine authorship and human authorship of the Bible while avoiding the errors of fundamentalism and liberalism. The Word of God, Bloesch says, is "not the text itself but the divinely intended meaning of the text. This meaning is hidden in the text, or, better, in the context of wider Scripture. The Word of God is the eternal wisdom of God—not to be equated with human wisdom, which is also reflected in the Bible."[30] In the biblical text we receive the revelation of God, but this revelation, the divinely intended meaning, can only be spiritually discerned.[31] Readers of Holy Scripture need a "revelational illumination" that draws them to the meaning of the text and enables them to hear God's Word in the text "directing us to the cross of Christ."[32] This is why Bloesch unites Word *and* Spirit explicitly in his hermeneutic.

Thus, we see a strong correlation between a doctrine of revelation, a theological hermeneutics (and of the meaning of *meaning*), with an understanding of the process of communication—from divine author to human recipients, readers of it in every age. Bloesch notes, "the reconstituted, critical orthodoxy that I am expounding views the Word as inseparable from the Bible, as its ground and goal. The Bible is reconceived as the divinely appointed means by which God makes his Word known to the church in every age."[33]

Thus, for Bloesch, "The revelational meaning of the text can be assessed not only by viewing the text in the context of the whole of Scripture but also by assessing the impact of this text on the faith of the church through the ages."[34]

8. The Fourfold Senses of Scripture: A Plurality of Meanings

Clement of Alexandria laid part of the groundwork for what would become a common fourfold distinction of meanings to be sought in Scripture.[35] He stated: "The meaning of the law is to be understood by us in four ways [one being the literal sense]: as displaying a sign, as establishing a command for right conduct, or as making known a prophecy."[36] The four ways would become more definitively known as the *literal*, the *allegorical*, the *moral*, and the *anagogical*, referring to future hope, eschatological development, or prophetic fulfillment.[37]

The following is an example of the fourfold senses of scriptural meaning. The city of Jerusalem is . . . (1) "Literal: a city in Palestine; the capital of Israel, (2) Allegorical (typological): the church militant here on earth, (3) Moral (tropological): the soul of the believer, (4) Mystagogical [or anagogical]: the heavenly city; the church triumphant."[38]

For Augustine, the difficulties that attended the literal interpretation of some Old Testament texts had served as a barrier to him believing Christianity to be true. He was relieved, on the path toward his ultimate conversion to Christ, to find a preacher in Ambrose who did not take everything in the Bible literally. As Augustine said in his *Confessions*, the autobiography of his conversion, "And I was delighted to hear Ambrose in his sermons to the people saying, as if he were most carefully enunciating a principle of exegesis: 'The letter kills, the spirit gives life' (2 Cor. 3:6). Those texts which, taken literally, seemed to contain perverse teaching he would expound spiritually, removing the mystical

Hermeneutics and Theological Interpretation

Types of Hermeneutics

veil."[39] For Augustine, the Bible offered itself to all readers in its simplicity, but its more seldom, difficult parts could be opened up and interpreted for edification by the skilled interpreter, who knew how to read by the analogy of faith.

The doctrine of multiple meanings, or multiple "senses" of Scripture, originated with Origen and was developed by Augustine and later by theologians and churchmen in the Middle Ages. The fourfold structure of biblical interpretation, which included the literal, allegorical, tropological (moral), and anagogical senses of Scripture's meaning, originated in the so-called "Alexandrian school" of interpretation. The Antiochene school focused on the literal sense of Scripture to the exclusion of the others.[40] The Reformation period, with Martin Luther and John Calvin, saw a return to the plain, literal sense of the text and the practice of a theological interpretation based in historical-grammatical exegesis.

9. Stephen Fowl: Interpretative Underdeterminacy

Stephen Fowl, in *Engaging Scripture*, names three alternatives in the practice of the interpretation of Scripture in relation to its "meaning": determinacy, indeterminacy, and underdeterminacy.[41] Those who practice a determinate interpretation view the text as having an ontological "meaning" that can be discerned through the correct interpretive practice. Those who hold to the indeterminacy of the text believe that the purpose of interpretation is to "upset, disrupt, and deconstruct interpretive certainties." Fowl's own position, underdeterminacy, is that no single method or interpretative strategy can claim epistemological superiority over any other. This position, he says, recognizes a plurality of interpretive communities that have their own interpretative practices. Underdeterminacy, Fowl claims, is the best way to approach the interpretation of Scripture because it avoids the errors of both determinacy and underdeterminacy and enables readings of the Bible that are faithful to its nature as Christian Scripture.

In Fowl's article, "The Ethics of Interpretation, or What's Left Over after the Elimination of Meaning," Fowl argues that because *meaning* is a term whose meaning depends largely on the context in which it is used. Because the criterion for determining whether one has arrived at the "meaning" of the text is governed by self-interest, it is better to dispense with the term *meaning* altogether.[42]

What counts as "meaning" in any given interpretation of a text will depend in large part on one's interpretative community, and the strategy one employs to derive "meaning" in the text.[43] Fowl refers to Jeffrey Stout's article in which he notes that "we really have no way of adjudicating between competing conceptions of textual meaning."[44] Fowl's proposal is that biblical scholars drop the term *meaning* and look at "these disputes in terms of interpretative interests."[45]

An interpreter's interest might be to discern an author's intentions in a text. But this strategy is not to uncover the meaning. This is in contrast to the work of E. D. Hirsch, who states that the meaning of a text must be tied to authorial intention. For Fowl, this may only tell us something about the text and something about the interpreter who finds value in that kind of interpretative strategy.

Dispensing with talk about the meaning of a text, Fowl suggests, provides interpreters with greater clarity regarding what it is they are looking for by way of interpretation, "what the reading is actually trying to achieve."[46]

This will not, Fowl points out, eliminate all disagreement within interpretative communities. Three areas of disagreement, he says, remain: (1) How do we articulate our interpretative interests? (2) How do we decide whether one's interpretative practice is adequate for achieving the goal? (3) Which "interpretative strategy" should we adopt?[47]

What follows from the elimination of "meaning" and the view that no interpretative interest can claim epistemological superiority over others? Within an interpretive strategy, different readings can achieve status as better and worse. Fowl finds three options: (1) the pluralist position, in which pluralism itself is the highest value; (2) the social responsibility view, which allows for some overarching criterion of helpful or harmful interpretative practices to the greater society;[48] and (3) the "communal or collective position" (the same as the social responsibility view, except that it "refuses to accept the two elements essential to the social responsibility position outlined above—a global polis and an

Types of Hermeneutics

ahistorical, trans-cultural, universally recognizable notion of justice."[49] Only a particular, historical interpretive community can provide criteria for better and worse, helpful or harmful interpretive strategies.

10. Reader-Response Hermeneutics: As Many Meanings as Readers (and Communities of Readers)	The postmodern skepticism toward the existence of absolute truth, of a God's-eye-view of the world, and of the possibility of apprehending and knowing truth outside of the truth that is "made" or "created" within community frameworks, extends to the issue of meaning. To the "masters of suspicion," an author can no longer claim authority over text. The meaning of the text is not confined to whatever the author wished or intended it to mean. In the postmodern perspective, readers create meaning in the act of interpreting a text. Since interpretations are historically conditioned anyway, and since readers cannot escape their own prejudices, biases, and points of view, they are free to interpret according to their own wishes, expectations, and interests. The deconstructionist turn in literary theory was not intended, by all practitioners, to bring negative and *destructive* results. Rather, some sought to bring attention to the fact that, because texts and readings and interpretations of texts are historically conditioned, they are often manipulated by those in power to keep society under wraps. Deconstruction teaches readers to say, "you think this means *that*, but it cannot mean *that*, because *that* is just a compilation of your historically and socially conditioned reality." Given, then, that all interpretations are communally, historically, and socially based, readers should attempt to interpret in ways that will benefit themselves, their communities, or overall society, depending on whatever the reader's priority of interest might be. Thus feminist literary criticism advocates the devaluation of patriarchal interpretive traditions and texts biased toward male headship in favor of interpretations favoring the liberation of women. Liberation theologies similarly advocate interpretations and theologies based on these interpretations that promote the liberation of the poor and the oppressed. Some postmodern reader-response traditions are extreme in the "violence" they do to the text and to the text's authors, while others try to find a place for the actual influence readers do have on texts, for the relative autonomy of texts as agents bearing meaning, and for the role of the author who constructed it. While reader-response hermeneutics rightly challenge the unhealthy dogmatism that can characterize overly prideful interpretive traditions as well as premature interpretive conclusions, they go too far in undermining the *authority* of a text original author, contextual setting, and other factors that should provide the boundaries for the meanings that readers discover in texts, even if those meanings do not accord with the readers' current interests, concerns, or paradigms.

Two Evangelical Approaches to Applying the Meaning of the Bible

Two evangelical theologians show the extremes in different philosophies of applying the Bible's meaning to contemporary issues and theological questions. Robert L. Thomas, in his book *Evangelical Hermeneutics*,[50] writes that the new evangelical approach to hermeneutics has turned from its conservative roots in its appropriation of hermeneutical insights from modern psychology, theology, and philosophy. He argues for a single, determinate meaning that can be discerned through the right application of historical-grammatical exegesis. William Webb proposes in his book *Slaves, Women and Homosexuals*[51] that the interpretation of Scripture needs to be approached methodologically, but also theologically, according to what he sees as a redemptive-historical trajectory in Scripture. This trajectory, he argues, while not always explicitly stated, is derived from Scripture itself. It would be a misreading of Scripture, according to Webb, to apply every text literally.

Nonhermeneutical Theology: Robert Thomas's Critique of the "New Evangelical Hermeneutics"

Thomas laments the increasing tide of change in evangelical hermeneutics, from the principle of the single, fixed meaning of every biblical utterance to variations allowing for multiple meanings (or submeanings) of words and sentences, Thomas suspects a connection in evangelical theology between the rising acceptability of psychology and a corresponding openness to the merits of secular philosophy for biblical hermeneutics. For Thomas, biblical hermeneutics can only be a "special hermeneutics," the interpretation and application of the meaning of the *Bible,* a text whose divine origin and content precludes much integration with secular disciplines.[52] Thomas holds that a word or sentence can have only one meaning, that which the original author intended, while a text's meaning may have additional or various applications in the present day. But Thomas states his preference for a distinction between interpretation, or discerning the meaning of a text, and application, applying that meaning to a contemporary situation. In reaction to those who advocate that the cultural situation of a reader can allow for a shift in perspective and thus in the meanings discerned in a text, Thomas writes, "Neither the culture of the interpreter nor the culture of the person to whom the interpreter communicates has anything in the world to do with the meaning of the biblical text. The meaning of the biblical text is fixed and unchanging. This is not to say that the exegetical task is finished. It must ever be open to new insights as to a more refined understanding of what the Spirit meant when He inspired the writers to pen Scripture, but that refined understanding must come through a closer utilization of the rules of grammar and the facts of history surrounding the text in its original setting. It is not open to a redefined understanding stemming from a reading back into the text of some consideration either from the interpreter's culture or from that of the one to whom the interpreter communicates."[53]

A Redemptive-Historical Hermeneutic: William Webb

Webb's book, *Slaves, Women and Homosexuals,* argues that in order to rightly apply the biblical text within our contemporary culture, and thus to speak to that culture, Christians need to differentiate between cultural components and transcultural components. The "cultural components" are "those aspects of the biblical text that we 'leave behind' as opposed to 'take with us' due to cultural differences between the text's world and the interpreter's world as we apply the text to subsequent generations."[54] For Webb, "cultural confinement" is "the gap between the world of the text and that of the interpreter, which requires a reapplication of the text."[55] Transcultural aspects of a text, then, would be that which reflects what Webb has called "kingdom values." A command such as "love your neighbor" is not freighted with cultural baggage such that it must be "left behind."[56] Webb's objective in this book is to "focus primarily on the criteria by which Christians can determine what is cultural and what is transcultural within Scripture."[57]

Webb's term *redemptive-movement hermeneutic* signifies that his approach to the application of Scripture is explicitly theological and consciously hermeneutical, taking into account the "redemptive spirit of the text."[58] It may not always be possible, Webb suggests, to fulfill the redemptive spirit of the text in one's application of it if the reader only lives out "the Bible's literal words in our modern context."[59] This latter hermeneutic Webb distinguishes the "redemptive-spirit appropriation of Scripture" from the "static appropriation of Scripture."

Charts *on* Prolegomena

Two Evangelical Approaches to Applying the Meaning of the Bible

"understands the words of the text aside from or with minimal emphasis upon their underlying spirit."[60] Webb argues that the redemptive movement "champions that which is of foremost importance for actualizing the sacred text today."[61]

Webb distances himself from hermeneutical approaches that are "progressive" in that they allow for new meanings to be brought to the biblical text from outside the Bible. Webb is concerned, rather, to show that redemptive-historical hermeneutics are derived from the biblical text and faithful to the trajectory established by the Bible writers within their cultural and social contexts. For Webb, there is an "ultimate ethic" to which the Scripture points, sometimes in ways that clearly reflect that ethic. At other times, for example, in some difficult Old Testament texts, that ethic may surface "only against the backdrop of the ancient culture."[62]

Christians, in our modern culture, should live out "the redemptive spirit that the text reflects as read against its original culture. . . . We need to move on, beyond the text, and take the redemptive dimension of those words further to a more redemptive level" (the ultimate ethic).[63]

In discerning the redemptive movement expressed in, and applicable from, a biblical text, Webb suggests that interpreters determine the relation between the text and the social environment to which and in which it speaks. If the movement it expresses is "preliminary," the "further movement in the direction set by the text would produce a more fully realized ethic."[64] If the movement in a particular text regarding an ethical matter is "absolute," then Scripture has provided the final, redemptive word on the issue. Modern interpreters need only apply the same absolute ethic given literally in Scripture to a similar situation today. For Webb, contemporary issues of gender (in particular the role of women in relation to that of men in the spheres of church and society) are reflected in Scripture by a "preliminary" movement; modern Christians can establish a more progressive and redemptive ethic with respect to the question of women and women's roles in society, home, and church. On the other hand, the issue of homosexuality is represented by an absolute movement in the Scriptures, so that Christians faithfully appropriate scriptural texts on homosexuality when they "continue its negative assessment of homosexual behavior and restrict such activity within the church, even if society at large does not."[65]

---

1. Benjamin Jowett, *On the Interpretation of Scripture, and Other Essays* (London: Routledge & Sons, 1907), 3.
2. Ibid., 6.
3. Ibid.
4. Ibid., 7.
5. E. D. Hirsch Jr., *Validity in Interpretation* (New Haven, CT: Yale University Press, 1967), 25.
6. Ibid., 213.
7. Ibid., 214.
8. Ibid., 255.
9. James Barr, "The Bible as Document of Believing Communities," in *The Bible as a Document of the University,* ed. Hans Dieter Betz (Atlanta: Scholars Press, 1981), 31.
10. Ibid., 35.
11. Francis Watson, *Text and Truth: Redefining Biblical Theology* (Grand Rapids: Eerdmans, 1997).
12. Ibid., 71.
13. Ibid.
14. Ibid.
15. Frank Kermode, *The Classic: Literary Images of Permanence and Change* (Cambridge, MA: Harvard University Press, 1975), 133.
16. Watson, *Text and Truth,* 73.
17. Ibid., 95.
18. Ibid.

Two Evangelical Approaches to Applying the Meaning of the Bible

19. Ibid., 97.
20. Ibid., 98.
21. Kevin J. Vanhoozer, *Is There a Meaning in This Text? The Bible, the Reader, and the Reality of Literary Knowledge* (Grand Rapids: Zondervan, 1998), 184.
22. Ibid., 187
23. In drawing this distinction Vanhoozer appeals to the work of E. D. Hirsch, such as *Validity in Interpretation.*
24. Ibid., 264.
25. Note the subjective interpretive methods of the "Jesus Seminar," in which members arbitrarily choose what are authentic or inauthentic sayings and events in Scripture.
26. Cf. R. K. Harrison, "Higher Criticism," in *Evangelical Dictionary of Theology,* ed. Walter A. Elwell (Grand Rapids: Baker, 1984).
27. A case could be made for placing Donald Bloesch's view just on the other side of our subjective/objective line. He has strong elements of subjectivity and objectivity in his hermeneutical approach. But we believe that his focus on meaning in the "mind of God" and on spiritual interpretation of divine meaning makes his view more subjective than objective.
28. Ibid., 200.
29. Donald Bloesch, *Holy Scripture: Revelation, Inspiration, and Interpretation* (Downers Grove, IL: InterVarsity Press, 1994), 212.
30. Ibid., 71.
31. Ibid.
32. Ibid., 202.
33. Ibid., 73.
34. Ibid., 192.
35. We place this view in the subjective camp because the history of allegorical interpretation has shown it to be a highly subjective endeavor, lacking objective hermeneutical controls. The literal level of interpretation has had a stronger history of "objectivity," or at least objectivity in principle. It was this level of interpretation, the literal, which Luther and the humanist Reformers wished to recapture.
36. Clement of Alexandria, *Stromata 1.28.3;* as cited in Alister McGrath, *The Christian Theology Reader* (Oxford: Blackwell, 2001), 78. The explanation in parentheses is McGrath's.
37. McGrath, *Christian Theology Reader,* 78.
38. Gerald Bray, *Biblical Interpretation: Past and Present* (Downers Grove, IL: InterVarsity Press, 1996), 147.
39. Augustine, *Confessions,* trans. Henry Chadwick (Oxford: Oxford University Press, 1991), 6.6.
40. See Kathryn Greene-McCreight, "Literal Sense," in *Dictionary for Theological Interpretation of the Bible,* ed. Kevin J. Vanhoozer, Craig G. Bartholomew, Daniel J. Treier, and N. T. Wright (Grand Rapids: Baker, 2005), 455–56.
41. Stephen Fowl, *Engaging Scripture* (Oxford: Blackwell, 1998), 10–11.
42. Stephen Fowl, "The Ethics of Interpretation, or What's Left Over after the Elimination of Meaning," in *The Bible in Three Dimensions: Essays in Celebration of Forty Years of Biblical Studies in the University of Sheffield,* ed. David J. A. Clines, Stephen E. Fowl, and Stanley E. Porter, Journal for the Study of the Old Testament Supplement Series 87 (Sheffield, England: Sheffield Academic Press, 1990).
43. Ibid., 379–80.
44. Jeffrey Stout, "What Is the Meaning of a Text?" *New Literary History* 14 (1982): 1–12.
45. Ibid., 380.
46. Ibid., 386.
47. Ibid., 388.
48. Ibid., 391.
49. Ibid., 395.

Hermeneutics and Theological Interpretation

Two Evangelical Approaches to Applying the Meaning of the Bible

50. Robert L. Thomas, *Evangelical Hermeneutics* (Grand Rapids: Kregel, 2002).

51. William Webb, *Slaves, Women and Homosexuals: Exploring the Hermeneutics of Cultural Analysis* (Downers Grove, IL: InterVarsity Press, 2001).

52. As an example of this integration of which Thomas disapproves, he mentions Anthony Thiselton's appropriation of Gadamer's hermeneutical insights in *Two Horizons: New Testament Hermeneutics and Philosophical Description* (Grand Rapids: Eerdmans, 1980).

53. Thomas, *Evangelical Hermeneutics*, 145.

54. Webb, *Slaves, Women and Homosexuals*, 24.

55. Ibid.

56. Ibid., 23.

57. Ibid., 25.

58. Ibid., 30.

59. Ibid.

60. Ibid.

61. Ibid., 31.

62. Ibid., 32.

63. Ibid., 33.

64. Ibid., 36.

65. Ibid., 39.

PART EIGHT
Faith and Reason

Faith and Reason

Different Views of the Relationship of Faith and Reason

	Reason Against Faith	Faith Seeking Understanding	Understanding Enabling Faith

Faith against reason and reason against faith represent extreme positions on the relation between faith, defined as Christian experiences of conversion that stem from and lead to a trust in God's special revelation, the Bible, and reason, the usually neutral capabilities of God's general revelation, represented mainly by the insights of philosophy and science. Faith seeking understanding and understanding enabling faith are moderate or even mediating positions and are usually "in-house" discussions within evangelical theology. There is surely much overlap, in the practice of theology, between these latter two positions.

Faith Against Reason	Reason Against Faith		

Faith Against Reason

Faith against reason assumes the "irrationality" of Christian faith in that it may be said to contradict human reason. That conflict, however, only provides evidence to the truth of Christianity, because human reason is inherently sinful and thus unable to grasp truth. Very early in Christianity, Tertullian asked the now-famous question: "What has Jerusalem to do with Athens?" He was reacting against the method of Justin Martyr and other early Christian apologists who were borrowing from pagan philosophy to construct Christian theology or to connect apologetically with pagan culture. On this view, where science, philosophy, and sociology appear to conflict with revelation, the resolution is easy: away with all but the Scriptures. In defending the full humanity of Christ against an early heretic, Tertullian wrote that the incarnation, death, and resurrection of the Son of God *as both fully human and fully divine* is to be believed "because it is absurd." This approach has been labeled "fideism." In this view, faith is essentially a blind leap into the dark. Faith is a matter of volition, or will, in which a person exerts the spiritual or emotive aspect of his or her being on the basis of the authority of revelation or of the Holy Spirit's effectual

Reason Against Faith

The reason against faith perspective prioritizes the conclusions and findings of reason (whether philosophy, sociology, or science) over the experience and reality of faith. Thus the authority of special/general revelation, the interpretive guidance of the church or tradition (creeds and confessions), and the experience of relating to God is trumped by the academic and professional elites. Much of the Enlightenment was a struggle to replace the prevailing Christian worldview (God as Creator and Governor of the world; Scripture as divinely given authority for faith and knowledge) with a philosophically and scientifically rational grid, in which God was pushed to the outskirts of relevance in matters of knowledge. The deists, who believed God created the world and then left it to its own devices, first prioritized reason in this way. Perhaps at the height of the modern consciousness, G. W. F. Hegel viewed God as the immanent world-historical Spirit, who was for a very long time explained in religious terms by the categories of Christianity. However, religious terms would ultimately be replaced by philosophical ones, as history progressed toward maturity.

Historical criticism or "higher criticism,"

Faith Seeking Understanding

Faith seeking understanding is driven by a conviction that theological truth (an understanding of God's revelation) is ultimately suprarational. It is not contrary to reason, but is *beyond* reason's ability to fully grasp and appropriate. Augustine commended the merits of pagan philosophy to help understand Scripture. He said Christians should plunder the Egyptians.[2] There are limits to what human reason can do, however, for Augustine. Faith must always be given primacy. We cannot reason our way directly to God, as if constructing a rational tower of Babylon. Anselm, taking up Augustine's insights, said that "faith seeks understanding." We really begin with faith, not with reason, in the process of knowing God and constructing theology. It may be that understanding in some way can strengthen faith, but it cannot, by itself, bring one to "stand at the threshold of faith."[3] Donald Bloesch, a contemporary representative of this view, holds to what he calls a "fideistic revelationism," in which "the relationship of faith and reason is not either-or but both-and; yet we must never fail to give priority to the first."[4]

This perspective provides a significant place for reason, and thus for philosophy, in

Understanding Enabling Faith

Whereas faith seeking understanding emphasizes the priority of special revelation (God revealed in the Incarnation, Scriptures, and the witness of the Holy Spirit), understanding enabling faith emphasizes general revelation. Paul, in Romans 1, tells us that God has revealed Himself through the things He has made, including making His presence known in the minds and moral consciousness of human creatures. Also, the presence of common grace in the world, God's good gifts to all His creation without respect to their relationship to Him, suggests that much can be gained by examining His imprints. An optimistic perspective on the ability of human reason to understand God and the Scriptures and to construct theology accordingly is given by representatives of this view. Thus, "natural law" is an important aspect of theology for proponents of this perspective. Thomas Aquinas, without doubt the most important theologian of the Middle Ages, represents this view with his "Five Ways," in *Summa Theologiae.* He sets out to prove the existence of God by examining the nature of certain aspects of the created order, such as cause and effect, possibility and necessity, aspects of "better and worse" in things, or "gradation," and the apparent design,

Faith and Reason

Different Views of the Relationship of Faith and Reason

Faith Against Reason	Reason Against Faith	Faith Seeking Understanding	Understanding Enabling Faith
call, and believes in the gospel and in God, against what natural reason would posit to be the case. Søren Kierkegaard is often incorrectly considered a representative of this view, given his several references to the Incarnation as the "absolute paradox." A paradox, as usually defined today, is only an "apparent contradiction," not a logical contradiction that demands a choice between two opposing alternatives. A better example of the fideist position might reside in elements of mysticism, in which the active engagement with God through the heart is superior to rational encounter. Postmodern theology bears some resemblance to fideism, with its community-constructed beliefs that may be internally but not externally rational. Their beliefs cohere within a structure and are believed by faith, but they do not correspond to external standards of reason that can be justified and held up to scrutiny.	in distinction from "lower criticism," which deals primarily with issues of text comparison, arose to prominence in academic theology in the late nineteenth century. It was a product of the Enlightenment worldview and was wedded to the Kantian distinction between that which can be known by reason, historical and scientific observation, and what can only be believed by faith. Historical criticism, at least in its interpretative approach to Scripture, emphasized that which can be known by reason to the exclusion of that which can be believed by faith. Thus while many proponents and practitioners of historical criticism made a place for faith in their personal lives, this was so far removed from their interpretation of Scripture and thus from their theology that it became difficult for faith to impinge upon interpretation of Scripture.	the task of theology. Reason has its limits, but we can draw upon it in our quest to increase our knowledge of God. The difficulty or challenge of this perspective is that it leaves the theologian with a tremendous responsibility to sift through philosophy and all other areas of human learning for that which will be of benefit. Not all philosophy, as Paul reminds us, is of benefit to the Christian life (Col. 2:8).	or inherent purpose, in things. Thomas logically deduces God's existence from these observations. This perspective is also represented in much of modern (in distinction from postmodern) apologetics, such as evidentialism (cf. Josh McDowell's *Evidence That Demands a Verdict*, for a popular version). Some contemporary examples of this position, in which Thomistic insights into "natural law" are heavily utilized, are expressed by evangelical theologians Norman Geisler and Gordon Clark. Theology that majors on the rational and logically and/or historically verifiable propositions of Scripture, represented in our contemporary period by Carl F. H. Henry, bears affinity to this perspective. This view can serve as a corrective to positions that do not adequately appreciate natural law, common grace, and general revelation. Also, theologians of this perspective rigorously address tough questions from skeptics. This perspective cannot retreat to private language games or coherentism, for it admits the ability of all thinkers to understand Christian concepts. Christianity is considered to be inherently rational and logical. However, this view can understate the need for conversion to fully understand Scripture. It can downplay the necessity of the Holy Spirit to guide people into truth.
Cornelius Van Till's presuppositionalist theology might be considered a form of fideism. While this perspective, in some forms, bears the merit of a strong conviction and a high view of the authority of Scripture or of tradition, it betrays a certain naïveté regarding the interpretation of Scripture. It undermines the significance of God's general revelation and its capability to guide people toward the truth. It also fails to recognize the capabilities of people outside of Christianity to arrive at some truth about the world and God, which might be beneficial even to	Rudolf Bultmann, in the field of New Testament studies, would apply the modern worldview to an existentialist interpretation, in which the Bible miracles would be "demythologized," or explained in terms more acceptable to modern, sophisticated people. We can no longer accept, he claimed, the conceptual categories under which the primitive peoples of the Bible were operating. While Bultmann meant to leave room for living, existential faith in the Christ of faith (not the Christ of history), one is left, under Bultmann's scheme, with a merely mythical and spiritual relationship to the world of the Bible. Under reason against faith, theology	Blaise Pascal, the great French philosopher and theologian of the seventeenth century, wrote of the famed "proofs" for God's existence (the cosmological, the teological, and the ontological) that they are "so remote from human reasoning, and so complex, that they have little impact. Even if they were of help to some people, this would only be for the moment during which they observed the demonstration, because an hour later, they would be afraid that they had deceived themselves."[5] For Pascal, the heart is the ultimate source of knowledge, not reason. The process of reasoning can only help us to recognize its limits. Things beyond reason are still objects of knowledge: "We know the truth, not only through our reason, but also through our heart. It is through this latter that we know first principles; and reason, which has nothing to do with this, vainly tries to refute them. The skeptics have no intention other than this; and they fail to achieve it."[6]	

Faith and Reason

Different Views of the Relationship of Faith and Reason

Faith Against Reason	Reason Against Faith	Faith Seeking Understanding	Understanding Enabling Faith
Christians. Finally, it proves unable to offer any "public," rational apologetic to a non-Christian. 1. Tertullian, "On the Flesh of Christ," in *Ante-Nicene Fathers*, ed. Alexander Roberts and James Donaldson, 2d ed. (reprint, Peabody, MA: Hendrickson, 1999), 3:525.	becomes mainly descriptive rather than prescriptive and normative. It does not tell us what is or what should be. It provides insights into the history of a religious people (Jews, Christians) and perhaps insights into how to develop religiosity when severely restricted by modern materialist assumptions.	2. Cf. Augustine's *On Christian Doctrine.* 3. Donald Bloesch, *A Theology of Word and Spirit: Authority and Method in Theology* (Downers Grove, IL.: InterVarsity Press, 1992), 36. 4. Ibid., 21, 61. 5. Blaise Pascal, *Pensees*, 446; cited in Alister McGrath, *A Christian Theology Reader* (Boston: Blackwell, 2001), 32. 6. Ibid., 110.	

PART NINE

The Source and Structure
of Truth

What Is Truth?

W*hat is Truth?* Pilate's query to Jesus is no less provocative and important a question today than it was in the first century. The question, when asked seriously, reflects humanity's innate desire to *know* what is true and to have right beliefs about ultimate reality, including God. In the arena of theology, truth is an issue of primary significance, if not *the* issue. If theology is the reasoned attempt to truly know God, ourselves, and the world conceptually and experientially, and if God *is* truth, then the question of truth for the theologian is primary.

But before, or at least *while*, the theologian asks whether accepted knowledge or belief is the truth, it is also necessary to ask what is meant by the concept of truth. Is truth a *quality* of a thing? Is it a designation of the relation between knowledge of something and that thing that is known? Is truth primarily the result of an activity, such as reason and rationality, or of experience and evidence? Is truth mainly a function of the exercise of a mind, or minds? Or is truth (or things that are true) independent of mind and consciousness? Is truth mainly subjective and personal? Is truth relative to time, location, and the knower? Finally, how does one justify that his or her knowledge and beliefs are "true"? These questions will be discussed in the following charts.

The Source and Structure of Truth

Nature of Truth

To ask about the nature of truth is not to ask what *is*, in fact, true. Discerning what is true is the task of metaphysics in philosophy and of theology proper. Rather, we are asking what theologians mean when they say they have arrived at a *true belief* about God or *true knowledge* of God? Is truth discovered or is it created? How is the quality "true" related to the activity of the mind? To the formulation of theological propositions? What is the structure under which truth is apprehended? To put it in a way that has immediate application to theology: "When asking about truth, we are specifically interested in finding what conditions a sentence, a statement, belief, or proposition must satisfy to be true."[1] Three basic views of the nature and structure of truth have been posited:[2] (1) truth as correspondence, (2) truth as coherence, and (3) truth as pragmatism.

1. Truth as Correspondence: Something (a belief, utterance, description, etc.) is true if it corresponds to "fact," or to reality as it actually is.	The perspective of truth as correspondence, though found in a variety of forms, has been a dominant understanding of the nature of truth throughout theological history. "Truth is correspondence with the facts" or "truth is agreement with reality."[3] Something is said to be true if whatever is purported or asserted, by whichever medium of communication (declarative statement, interrogative utterance, scientific conclusion, etc.), adequately represents reality *as it actually is*. A statement, a belief, or a depiction is true if it sufficiently and adequately represents to its context the state of affairs to which it refers. One might say that a correspondence theory of truth gives less importance to the search for knowledge through theology, science, or philosophy, and epistemology than to ontology (the study of existence) or to metaphysics (the study of nonphysical reality). This is because the disciplines (or mediums) that attempt to acquire and/or apprehend knowledge are seeking after something that lies "out there," beyond the bounds of finite knowing and finite abilities to grasp truth completely and entirely. Several objections have been raised against the correspondence perspective. The one we will deal with here is directed against that form of the theory that envisions correspondence as a "picturing relation." A sentence, proposition, assertion, and so forth correspond to reality in that it depicts or pictures what is. "George W. Bush is the president of the United States" is a statement that can be said to rightly "picture" the present state of America's governmental leadership. However, not all statements or assertions "picture" states of affairs. Statements in the subjunctive mood ("I would go to town if I had enough money.") do not "picture" a single state of affairs existing in the actual world. "Normative" statements, which give a command or a directive to someone, do not necessarily "picture" a state of affairs, but they may actually *bring about* a state of affairs in the actual world if they are obeyed.[4] "Pass the ketchup" does not picture a state of affairs; rather it creates the possibility of a new state of affairs, if the ketchup is passed. Work in the philosophy of language has focused attention on "performative utterances." These are statements that do, in fact, bring about a new state of affairs simply by virtue of the utterance being made by the proper authority in the appropriate situation. When the priest or minister pronounces a man and a woman "husband and wife," he or she does not "picture the world" by the statement; rather a new situation is created by the performative utterance. In theology, this distinction encourages the interpreter of Scripture, for example, to not simply read the Bible as a collection of propositions that "picture" a state of affairs, but to be attentive to ways in which the biblical text may contain "performative utterances" that are true in that they bring about a new reality. Nonetheless, in theology, a correspondence view of truth holds to the importance of representing God insofar as He has made Himself known and insofar as the possibility for knowing Him is available to the human mind. Theologians who hold to correspondence theories of truth draw on a variety of sources for acquiring knowledge, including revelation (special and divine), reason, experience, and authoritative statements. Protestant theologies, particularly evangelical, typically focus on the priority of special revelation for acquiring knowledge that corresponds to ultimate reality. Some theologians are more optimistic than others regarding the nature of that knowledge as it *corresponds* to God's own knowledge. For some theologians, we can only acquire an indirect, an analogical, or a metaphorical knowledge of God. For others, God has so manifested Himself in His revelation that any true knowledge of Him and of the world will be fundamentally equal to the knowledge that He has of those things, albeit the *amount* of knowledge He possesses is still infinitely more than ours could ever be.

The Source and Structure of Truth

Nature of Truth

In the main, evangelical theologies have held to some form of the correspondence theory of truth. Evangelical theologians who empathize with the postmodern critiques of the modernist quest for indubitable certainty in knowledge have been more prone to reject—or at least modify—some aspects of correspondence in favor of coherence or pragmatist notions.

2. Truth as Coherence: Something (a belief, utterance, description, etc.) is true if it can be verified—shown to be logically, systematically, or pragmatically entailed or justified—by its "fit" in a belief system of related and interconnected truths.

W. V. O. Quine, in response to foundationalism as a system of verification for meaning and justification for truth, described the nature of truth (and belief) using the metaphor of a "web." Rather than a structural metaphor, such as a building or a pyramid, in which subordinate truths are entailed logically by more fundamental truths, Quine saw each belief as equally necessary and no more foundational than any other. So long as they exist in one's belief structure, each part serves equally to validate the whole, and the whole serves to validate the parts.[5]

Pointing out the flaws in the correspondence theory of truth and, specifically, the foundational approach of René Descartes, in which immediate ideas (perceptions) give rise to mediate ideas in a very abstract sense, Harold Joachim emphasized the "concreteness" of the coherence notion of truth, "as a living and moving whole."[6] He defined the theory as "that systematic coherence which is the character of a significant whole. A 'significant whole' is an organized individual experience, self-fulfilling and self-fulfilled."[7]

He pointed out that correspondence (between perceptions and ideas with reality) may be a symptom of the truth, but it does not serve to sufficiently describe the nature of truth.[8]

Truth, for Joachim, is always mind dependent because it is apprehended by finite knowers in a finite world. According to the correspondence view of truth, "We do not make or alter truth by our thinking." But, for Joachim, "Truth, if it is to be *for me*, must enter into my intellectual endeavour and emerge in my conscious thought as the result of a personal process, and as, in a sense, my personal possession. I must get to know it, and I must express it when known, and the expression is tinged with my personal individuality and is my judgement."[9] While truth may be, in and of itself, independent, "this independent truth lives and moves and has its being in the judgements of finite minds."[10]

Joachim's coherence view of truth was influenced by that of G. W. F. Hegel, and thus was universal, single, and timeless, though apprehended differently throughout the world's historical development. Essentially, *all truth* coheres in a seemingly single, overarching system, though expressed and articulated differently by various individuals.

In the postmodern situation, truth as coherence has been received by many as the best way to describe the nature of truth and the acquisition of truth. The postmodern view of coherence, however, differs from that expressed by Joachim. For many influenced by the philosophical and cultural notions of postmodernism, truth is not a universal, ultimate phenomenon; rather, it is a designation for a communally agreed-upon standard of explaining the nature of reality, of God, or of how people ought to behave within a given community. That is, one could be said to believe something *truly* if what one believes represents and is validated by the local community of which one is a part. Beliefs and actions, then, *cohere* within the structure of language, culture, meaning, and reality established by a particular community.

Stanley Grenz, preferring a more holistic vision of theology's task than has been commonly represented by evangelicalism's doctrinal propositionalism, has sought to expand on the insights of George Lindbeck, whose "cultural-linguistic" view of religion likened religions to languages and religious doctrine to grammar. Grenz sought to revise evangelical theology in light of the current demands and appropriated insights of postmodernity, while also attempting to remain faithful to the best of Christian tradition as its resources for theological authority.[11]

Grenz sees the task of theology as a second-order discipline, that of reflecting on the experiences of being the people of God. Grenz, unlike the propositionalist theologians, sees theological doctrine as not an *a priori*, purely rational discipline that leads to experience. Rather, the experience of the people of God in the local (and time-specific) Christian community, informed by the work of the Holy Spirit in personal conversion and in the interaction with the community of faith, leads to doctrinal understandings. Grenz envisions theological truth as a mosaic, with narratives, symbols, and images filling out the picture of what God is doing with and in His people.

The Source and Structure of Truth

Nature of Truth

This theology must be practical as well as propositional, communal as well as individual, reality. The ultimate nature of and apprehension of truth is *holistic*. He states, "The contemporary situation demands that we as evangelicals not view theology merely as the restatement of a body of propositional truths, as important as doctrine is. Rather, theology is a practical discipline oriented toward the believing community. . . . Our participation in a faith community involves a basic commitment to a specific conceptual framework. Because faith is linked to a conceptual framework, our participation in a community of faith carries a claim to truth, even if that claim be merely implicit. By its very nature, the conceptual framework of a faith community claims to represent in some form the truth about the world and the divine reality its members have come to know and experience. To the extent that it embodies the conceptual framework of a faith community, therefore, theology necessarily engages in the quest for truth. It enters into conversation with other disciplines of human knowledge with the goal of setting forth a Christian worldview that coheres with what we know about human experience in the world."[12]

Recognize that Grenz has not said that there is no truth "out there" apart from the communities' perceptions of it. Nor is he saying that theological propositions have no ontological import, or do not describe ultimate reality. He is suggesting, rather, that there is no actual and existential perception of truth apart from that which is mediated to persons through the experience of life in community, including the testimony of Scripture, as it is interpreted and taught by a community. For Grenz, the best way to understand truth (and thus the best way to understand the task and objectives of theology) is not as the correspondence between a proposition and the reality it represents, but rather as a dynamic, holistic mosaic that incorporates all the elements of existence and reality in a single whole.

There is not one sole authority, such as Scripture, or doctrinal tradition, to which one can refer in seeking truth. Rather, God has made Himself known in numerous ways in our finite existence. Scripture testifies to the Word of God and thus mediates God's Word to its readers/ hearers. We employ and appeal to every possible avenue in which we might apprehend the truth of God and thus "gain our identity as the people of God."[13]

3. Truth as Pragmatism: Something is true if it brings about desirable results.

Truth as pragmatism is the view that truth is a correlate of that which works to bring about a desired result in the cognitive task of seeking truth. William James, a well-known American pragmatist whose classic work *The Varieties of Religious Experience* laid much of the groundwork for a psychological and individualistic study of religion, adhered to the "instrumentalist theory" of pragmatism. For James, "a proposition counts as true if an only if behaviour based on a belief in the proposition leads, in the long run and all things considered, to beneficial results for the believers."[14]

At points James seemed to agree with a measure of truth as correspondence. He states, "Truth, as any dictionary will tell you, is a property of certain of our ideas. It means their 'agreement,' as falsity means their disagreement, with 'reality.' Pragmatists and intellectualists both accept this definition as a matter of course. They begin to quarrel only after the question is raised as to what may precisely be meant by the term "agreement," and what by the term "reality" when reality is taken as something for our ideas to agree with.[15]

James disagreed with the "intellectualists" or rationalists who insisted, in his opinion, that truth is an "inert static relation." For these rationalists, "When you've got your true idea of anything, there's an end of the matter. You're in possession; you *know*; you have fulfilled your thinking destiny. . . . Pragmatism, on the other hand, asks its usual question. 'Grant an idea or belief to be true,' it says, 'what concrete difference will its being true make in any one's actual life? How will the truth be realized? What experiences will be different from those which would obtain if the belief were false? What, in short, is the truth's cash-value in experiential terms?'"[16]

For James, truth is not a static or inert "property"; rather, truth is something that "happens to an idea." Truth is verified through a process or event in which the cash value of an idea or belief is made clear to the one holding that idea.[17]

So James: "Our account of truth is an account of truths in the plural, of processes of leading . . . and having only this quality in common,

Nature of Truth

that they *pay*. Truth for us is simply a collective name for verification-processes, just as health, wealth, strength, etc., are names for other processes connected with life, and also pursued because it pays to pursue them. Truth is *made*, just as health, wealth and strength are made, in the course of experience."[18]

Long after James, George Lindbeck's *The Nature of Doctrine* set the agenda for what is called "postliberal" theology. In this work, Lindbeck seeks to articulate a vision for understanding religion and religious doctrine in a framework that would facilitate ecumenical unity among Christian denominations while encouraging distinctive traditions to retain their unique—and seemingly opposed—doctrinal formulations.

Lindbeck identifies two prevailing models for understanding and conceptualizing religion, the cognitivist and the experiential expressivist. He presents a third, the cultural linguistic, which he endorses as the best way (the most pragmatic) to conceive of religion.

Cognitivist views of religion and doctrine prioritize propositional and scientific approaches to apprehending objective truth, while experiential-expressivist models of religion are grounded on the conviction that a universal experience (though experienced particularly in ecclesial community) of the transcendent and the divine (cf. Friedrich Schleiermacher) gives rise, consequently, to the expression of that experience through religious symbols, art, doctrines, and ethics.

In contrast, the cultural-linguistic view suggests that the religious symbols and doctrines come before, and give rise to, the particular religious experience of those symbols. Thus religions serve to provide a conceptual structure whereby an adherent to the particular religion *becomes* and *believes* what is prescribed within the linguistic (doctrinal) convictions of that particular faith community or tradition. So Lindbeck: "Religion cannot be pictured in the cognitivist (and voluntarist) manner as primarily a matter of deliberately choosing to believe or follow explicitly known propositions or directives. Rather, to become religious—no less than to become culturally or linguistically competent—is to interiorize a set of skills by practice and training. One learns how to feel, act, and think in conformity with a religious tradition that is, in its inner structure, far richer and more subtle than can be explicitly articulated. The primary knowledge is not *about* the religion, nor *that* the religion teaches such and such, but rather *how* to be religious in such and such ways."[19]

Thus, for Lindbeck, truth is given in cultural-linguistic communities, and religious doctrinal truth teachings exist for a pragmatic function: They are rules of ethical guidance, belief-content, as well as structure on which to build religious experience and meaning in one's faith and existence.

Though we have rightly placed Lindbeck as illustrative of a pragmatic understanding of truth, this view is close to the idea of truth as coherence. Its emphasis is on the emergence and apprehension of truth as that which derives from a particular community of faith, belief, and practice. Indeed, one notes several points shared between Lindbeck and Grenz's revision of evangelical theology in this respect.

1. Paul K. Moser, Dwayne H. Mulder, and J. D. Trout, *The Theory of Knowledge: A Thematic Introduction* (New York: Oxford University Press, 1998), 60.
2. P. Hor, "Truth," in *Cambridge Dictionary of Philosophy*, ed. Robert Audi (Cambridge, England: Cambridge University Press, 1999), 931. Some authors include "relativism" as one theory of the nature of truth. Relativists hold that "truth" is always justified by and determined by individual persons, communities, and the local situation under which the knower works. For a helpful explanation of relativism, see Moser, Mulder, and Trout, *Theory of Knowledge*, 61–64.
3. Richard L. Kirkham, "Truth, correspondence theory of," in *Routledge Encyclopedia of Philosophy*, ed. Edward Craig (New York: Routledge, n.d.).
4. See Moser, Mulder, and Trout, *Theory of Knowledge*, 66–67.
5. Cf. John E. Thiel, *Nonfoundationalism* (Minneapolis: Fortress, 1991) for a helpful explanation of the influence of Quine's nonfoundational philosophy on contemporary theology.
6. Ibid, 77.
7. Harold H. Joachim, *The Nature of Truth* (reprint, New York: Greenwood, 1969), 76.
8. Ibid, 19.

The Source and Structure of Truth

Nature of Truth

9. Ibid., 21.
10. Ibid., 21–22.
11. Stanley Grenz, *Revisioning Evangelical Theology* (Downers Grove, IL: InterVarsity Press, 1993).
12. Ibid., 79.
13. Ibid., 136.
14. Richard L. Kirkham, "Pragmatic Theory of Truth," in *Routledge Encyclopedia of Philosophy*, 478–80.
15. William James, *Pragmatism and Other Essays* (New York: Washington Square, 1963), 88.
16. Ibid.
17. Ibid., 89
18. Ibid., 96.
19. George Lindbeck, *The Nature of Doctrine: Religion and Theology in a Postliberal Age* (Philadelphia: Westminster, 1984), 35.

How Can We Come to Have "True" Theological Knowledge?

Two facets of truth have commonly been held: truth of being and truth of knowing. The former relates to how objects in the world correspond to "the exemplar or idea on which it depends."[20] The latter, truth of knowing, is the "knowing conformity of mind to being." It is the exercise of "judgment" regarding the perceived case of things.[21] Epistemology is the attempt at verifying the judgments, the knowledge, that one has. In this next section, we compare various ways in which theologians have believed that we come to acquire truth with respect to our knowledge.

20. Thomas C. O'Brien, "Truth," in *Encyclopedic Dictionary of Religion*, ed. Paul Kevin Meagher, Thomas C. O'Brien, and Consuelo Maria Aherne (Washington, DC: Corpus, 1979), 3577.
21. Ibid.

Rational Evidentialism	Revelational Presuppositionalism	Rational and Propositional Revelationalism	Fideistic Revelationalism[40]
Rational evidentialism regards truth as a characteristic of a claim, the merits of which are determined by whether evidence or experience can validate an assertion or hypothesis. Much of Enlightenment theology was driven by the desire for empirical verification. Theology was to be "queen of the sciences." Evidential theologies generally focused more on the merits of natural theology than on that of revealed theology (at least for apologetic purposes), since the data of natural theology, it was assumed, can be more easily and visibly verified. Not all evidentially minded theologians hold to the superiority of natural theology or natural things to revealed content (e.g., Scripture), but all would assert the importance of evidence and reason to supplement, support, clarify, and explain the data and meaning of revelation. After all, everything and all matters of evidence are created by God. Even the ability to reason can be seen as an "evidence" for God's existence. However, the evidential turn of modernity also made its way into the data of revelation, giving rise to the predominance in some theological circles on the European continent, and later in England and America, of the	Cornelius Van Til suggested that the knowledge of God and of the world, in the sense that *God* knows it, is essentially unavailable to unaided fallible humans. However, through special revelation, God has made truth known to humanity. This truth is ascertainable and knowable by Christians in analogy. Humanity's knowledge of God is thus a derivative knowledge and is thus not equal with God's knowledge, which is "self-contained" knowledge.[26] Van Til explains, "By this is meant that God is the original and that man is the derivative. God has absolute self-contained system within himself. What comes to pass in history happens in accord with that system or plan by which he orders the universe. But man, as God's creature, cannot have a replica of that system of God. He cannot have a reproduction of that system. He must, to be sure, think God's thoughts after him; but this means that he must, in seeking to form his own system, constantly be subject to the authority of God's system *to the extent* that this is revealed to him."[27] Van Til is concerned with a prevailing tendency in modern theology to see humanity "as the final reference point" and thus the final	For Carl F. H. Henry, "The God of biblical revelation is the God of reason, not Ultimate Irrationality; all he does is rational."[35] Henry does not assert, however, the supremacy of reason in coming to understand and know God. Rather, God can only be known truly through the revelation of Himself, which He has provided in Scripture. As he states, "Be they gods of secular philosophy or gods of the history of religion, the false gods can in principle be completely known for what they are simply through human inquiry and ingenuity. Given enough time and effort, any person can explore, expound and expose the nature of these 'divinities.' . . . But to speak of God and attribute specific characteristics to him apart from a basis in divine revelation is to play the gardener who, after spraying water into the sky from a hose, then welcomes the 'rainfall' as 'heaven-sent.'"[36] For Henry, divine revelation takes the form of propositions. God communicates His nature, actions, and purposes through the meaningful, truthful (and inerrant) statements and stories of Scripture. That is, God communicates true *information* about Himself to the recipients of revelation. This communication,	Karl Barth insisted that there is no "point of contact" between humanity and the Word of God. God's revelation of Himself always comes to a humanity that cannot naturally receive and understand it. There is no "capability or property grounded in man," by or through which the experience of God's revelation in Christ, preaching, and Scripture can take place.[41] When theology expresses a real knowledge of God, it is because the Word of God has entered into the theologian's reality, making him or her a witness of the truth of that reality. When one has truly heard the Word of God, "there can be no question of any ability to hear or understand or know on his part, of any capability that he the creature, the sinner, the one who waits, has to bring to this Word, but that the possibility of knowledge corresponding to the real Word of God has come to him, that it represents an inconceivable *novum* compared to all his ability and capability, and that it is to be understood as a pure fact, in exactly the same way as the real Word of God itself."[42] When one experiences the reality of the Word, one believes, not on the basis of evidence, reason,

The Source and Structure of Truth

How Can We Come to Have "True" Theological Knowledge?

Rational Evidentialism	Revelational Presuppositionalism	Rational and Propositional Revelationalism	Fideistic Revelationalism
historical criticism of the Bible. Miracles, since they cannot be historically verified, were deemed by some to be epistemically unjustified. If they were to be believed literally, it must be on the strength of blind faith alone ("fideism"). E. L. Mascall, in *The Openness of Being*, writes a moderate defense of natural theology in which he upholds the importance of metaphysical reflection on the natural world, both empiricism and rationality, for Christian theology. He does not argue for the superiority of empiricism or rationalism in theology, but for the significance for it in theology: "Because I believe that God has created man as a rational animal and has endowed him with natural powers, of which reason itself is one of the most significant, I hold that in religious experience there is a common element which is highly important and which can be brought under rational examination. Furthermore, because I believe that all natural objects have the common characteristic of being created and sustained by God, I hold that rational investigation of them may disclose rational grounds for believing in his existence."[22] In evangelical circles, one also thinks of evidentialism in the realm of apologetics.[23] In evidentialism, traditional arguments for the existence of God (e.g., ontological, Aquinas's "five ways"), references to historical and archaeological findings that verify the data of Scripture, and logical and scientific	source of knowledge.[28] However, any epistemology that makes humanity, rather than God, its ultimate reference point cannot offer an optimistic account of the possibility of knowing anything at all. For Van Til, "The final reference point in predication is God as the self-sufficient One."[29] Thus the only true Christian epistemology is one that posits the existence of the Triune God that revealed Himself through Holy Scriptures. This epistemology, what Van Til calls "The Reformed method of apologetics . . . begins frankly 'from above.' It would 'presuppose' God."[30] The only way that the data of the world, of reason, and of our experience can be rightly interpreted is in light of the order (and "system") in which the God of the universe has placed it. As he states, "Reason and fact cannot be brought into fruitful union with one another except upon the presupposition of the existence of God and his control over the universe."[31] How is God's system, including His presence and work in the world and thus His truth, to be learned and rightly understood? Only through the Scriptures: "Accordingly, the Bible must be identified in its entirety in all that it says on any subject as the Word of God. It is, again, only if history is considered to be what it is because of the ultimate controlling plan of God, that such a relationship between God's Word and all the facts of the universe can be obtained."[32] Van Til's presuppositionalism is not a	this information, is not itself salvific, but is the precondition for salvation. It is necessary first to know *about* God before one can *know* God. By making this distinction, Henry set his view of biblical truth (what we have called "propositional revelationism") apart from the existential theologies that had achieved fashion in various theological circles. They held that revelation was synonymous with redemption: truth is *personal*, not *propositional*. It effects a new reality, a new relation with God, rather than providing information about God. Nonetheless, As James Emery White points out, Henry would deny being an adherent of a correspondence theory of truth, because he did not wish to align himself with the evidential approach to apologetics. This does not mean, however, that Henry does not believe in ultimate truth to which our apprehensions of it correspond. White states, "While Henry would deny being an adherent of a correspondence theory of truth, his resistance to that label is epistemological, not ontological, in orientation. . . . What Henry ultimately offers is a modification of the correspondence theory of truth."[37] White says that for Henry, our knowledge of reality is not a correspondence in that our knowledge is distinct from the reality it knows. Rather, Henry's correspondence theory is "an understanding of truth in terms of divine revelation, which gives us reality in true correspondence." Whatever God reveals, we can know it just as God knows it.	or internal ability, but because of the faith that has been created in him or her by transformative encounter with revelation. Barth emphasizes the freedom of God in revealing Himself through His Word to sinful, finite people: "The fact of God's Word does not receive its dignity and validity in any respect or even to the slightest degree from a presupposition that we bring to it. Its truth for us, like its truth in itself, is grounded absolutely in itself. . . . Men can know the Word of God because and in so far as God wills that they know it, because and in so far as there is or over against God's will only the impotence of disobedience . . ."[43] Donald Bloesch, a theological successor of Barth's, in *A Theology of Word and Spirit*, states that to recover biblical, evangelical theology, one must adhere neither to presuppositionalism, foundationalism, evidentialism, nor coherentism. Rather, he affirms *fideistic revelationism*, "in which the decision of faith is as important as the fact of revelation in giving us certainty of the truth of faith."[44] Bloesch employs Barth's emphasis upon the freedom of God to speak His Word to humanity, apart from human *a priori* assumptions, universal principles, or transcendental ideals. Bloesch wishes to maintain a proper unity between the subjective and objective elements of theology, while keeping the sovereignty of God, and His revelation, in its proper place over the insights of anthropology.

The Source and Structure of Truth

Charts *on* Prolegomena

How Can We Come to Have "True" Theological Knowledge?

Fideistic Revelationalism	Rational and Propositional Revelationalism	Revelational Presuppositionalism	Rational Evidentialism
For Bloesch, "In a theology of Word and Spirit we receive or hear the concrete speech of God, which makes an indelible impression on the human soul but can never be fully assimilated by the human mind. To know the full import of what is revealed, we must act in obedience to what we presently ascertain to be the will of God."[45] For Bloesch, if there is any "foundation," in the philosophical, epistemological sense of the word, of theology, it is God Himself, not sense impressions or "non-inferential beliefs." However, theology is concerned with truth, and with making and validating the truth claims of revelation. Yet these claims are ascertained and understood in existence, faith, and obedience. Thus experience and obedience enables interpretation and understanding, and interpretation and understanding enables obedience.	Gordon Clark, another proponent of rational, revelational propositionalism, says that "knowledge . . . requires an existing object, and that object is truth—truth that always has and always will exist."[38] For Clark, "the object of knowledge is a proposition, a meaning, a significance; it is a thought. And this is necessary if communication is to be possible. . . . The truths or propositions that may be known are the thoughts of God, the eternal thought of God. And insofar as man knows anything, he is in contact with God's mind."[39]	strict fideism, though at times it sounds like it. Rather, his view of truth depended heavily on the regenerative power of the Holy Spirit and the convincing strength of the Word of God. As he states, "It is through the heavenly content of the Word that God speaks of himself. Faith is not blind faith; it is faith in the truth, the system of truth displayed in the Scriptures."[33] James Emery White has pointed out that Van Til "sought to avoid a correspondence concept of truth that allowed correspondence between an object and an idea and gave independent significance to either one." Rather, both are part of a system of reality that must be presupposed before knowledge of any of the parts can be made known.[34]	arguments for the reasonableness of a literal creation seek to provide the unbeliever with reasons to believe in Christianity or, at the least, to remove obstacles in his or her path to so believing. Phillip Johnson has studied in-depth the intersection of theology and science. He has argued for the evidential coherence and rationality of a Christian view of creation against the prevailing views of evolutionary science. He has drawn on traditional arguments for the existence of God, such as the argument from design,[24] as well as on contemporary findings in science to make a case for the reasonableness of Christianity in the modern context.[25]

Fideistic Revelationalism

40. This is Donald Bloesch's name for his own approach to the theological task. Cf. Bloesch, A Theology of Word and Spirit (Downers Grove, IL: InterVarsity Press, 1992), 21.
41. Karl Barth, Church Dogmatics, 2d ed., ed. G. W. Bromiley and T. F. Torrance (Edinburgh: T & T Clark, 1975), 1:193.
42. Ibid., 194.
43. Ibid., 196.
44. Bloesch, Theology of Word and Spirit, 21.
45. Ibid., 22.

Rational and Propositional Revelationalism

35. Carl F. H. Henry, God, Revelation and Authority, 4 vols. (Waco, TX: Word, 1976–82), 1:233.
36. Ibid., 19.
37. White, What Is Truth? 104.
38. Gordon Clark, A Christian View of Men and Things (Grand Rapids: Eerdmans, 1952), 318–19. See also Clark's Language and Theology (Jefferson, MD: Trinity Foundation, 1980).
39. Clark, A Christian View, 321.

Revelational Presuppositionalism

26. Cornelius Van Til, Apologetics (Philadelphia: Westminster Theological Seminary, 1971), 9.
27. Cornelius Van Til, A Christian Theory of Knowledge (Philadelphia: Presbyterian & Reformed, 1969), 16.
28. Ibid., 17.
29. Ibid.
30. Ibid., 18.
31. Ibid.
32. Ibid., 31.
33. Ibid., 33.
34. James Emery White, What Is Truth? (Nashville: Broadman & Holman, 1994). White refers to Scott Olliphant's "The Consistency of Van Til's Methodology," Westminster Theological Journal 52.1 (Spring 1990): 35.

Rational Evidentialism

22. E. L. Mascall, The Openness of Being: Natural Theology Today (Philadelphia: Westminster, 1971), 4.
23. Cf. Josh McDowell, Evidence That Demands a Verdict: Historical Evidences for the Christian Faith (San Bernardino, CA: Campus Crusade for Christ, 1972). An updated version was published in 1999 by Thomas Nelson.
24. See his article, Phillip Johnson, "Is There a Blind Watchmaker?" in Reason in the Balance: The Case Against Naturalism in Science, Law and Education (Downers Grove, IL: InterVarsity Press, 1995).
25. See also Phillip Johnson, The Right Questions: Truth, Meaning and Public Debate (Downers Grove, IL: InterVarsity Press, 2002).

The Source and Structure of Truth

The Source of Truth

Rationalism	Empiricism	Authoritative Revelation

Rationalism

Rationalism is characteristic of the modern era, deriving largely from the Enlightenment emphasis upon reason and human rationality to acquire and apprehend truth. Human rationality was a conscious source for theology, from the Patristic period through the Medieval era and Reformation. But it was, at least theoretically, subordinate as the arbiter or instrument whereby revelation, whether general or special, was understood, interpreted, and appropriated. In the modern period, reason took on a much more significant role, becoming in many cases a substitute for revelation or a determinant of what *could be* a divine revelation in the first place.

René Descartes, who reasoned, *Cogito ergo sum* ("I think therefore I am"), is a founder of modern rationalism. He attempted to ground all of his beliefs and understandings of God and reality in a deductive, rational process. His attempt was not so much to usurp religion with rationalism, but the current and tide that stemmed from his philosophy turned much of traditional theology upside down.

Much of conservative evangelical theology in the modern period is known, in contradistinction from existential-experiential, mystical, or even some neo-orthodox theologies, for its emphasis on the importance of maintaining rationally coherent, publicly defensible, and logically explicable theological methodologies.

Empiricism

Whereas rationalism appeals to universal rules of logic or the derivations of internal reasoning, empiricism finds the source of truth to lie primarily in experience and observation, whether sense experience, scientific observations, or intuition. Where rationalism relies on deductive reasoning and logic (a truth is entailed by the structure of a proposition: "All bachelors are unmarried men. John is an unmarried man. Therefore John is a bachelor."), empiricism relies on inductive argumentation. The empiricist examines the available and relevant evidence and derives a conclusion from the ground up.

Empiricism came about in reaction to the rising tide of Enlightenment rationalism, largely through David Hume (cf. *An Enquiry Concerning Human Understanding*), whose skepticism challenged the ideals of rationalism to prove by evidence what they could only exclaim by logical syllogism. The data of sensation must be the primary source of our concepts for them to have meaning.[46]

Empiricism takes any of several forms in theology, including liberal theology's insistence upon human experience of the divine as the ground and source of religious truth. Friedrich Schleiermacher's theology, with its centering on the "feeling of absolute dependence" as the source and ground of ecclesial piety and communion, is probably the best example of this kind of empiricism in modern theology.

---

46. Cf. Moser, Mulder and Trout, *Theory of Knowledge,* 106–7.

Authoritative Revelation

No theologian would discount the significance of reason or experience. One must employ the best of reasoning and of experimentation. Reason is necessary to make sense of experience and experimentation, and experience is necessary in order to have data with which to reason.

But many theologians give first place, in terms of theological data, to revelation. As noted, revelation can take the form of a general or natural revelation, or special or supernatural revelation. But whereas science, history, philosophy, sociology, and other disciplines can disregard, for the most part, the phenomenon of divine revelation and of humanity's experience of that revelation, theology is largely driven by revelation.

It would be difficult to find theologians who pay no heed at all to revelation in some form. Certainly there are those who are more prominently driven by the data of reason or empiricism than by revelation as a normative source. Such theologians follow to the Enlightenment and the ethos of Modernity. Their emphasis is upon reason or experience as a way to free theology from the constraints of ecclesial authority.

Thus the issue of revelation as a theological source becomes also an issue of authority. The differences lie not so much with answers to the question of whether revelation should have anything to say at all to our modern situation. Rather the disagreements concern *how* and *in what manner* that revelation should be interpreted and appropriated to contemporary life. So the debate returns to *what kind of authority* revelation has in the theological task and to what extent does the worldview represented in Scripture become normative in the current situation.

Differences remain between the Protestant and Catholic churches on the issue of revelation as authority and data for truth. Whereas Protestants, at least in principle, see special revelation of Scripture as the ultimate and supreme—though

The Source and Structure of Truth

The Source of Truth

Authoritative Revelation	Empiricism	Rationalism
not *only*—source of truth, Roman Catholics see the role of the ecclesial church to be an equal bearer of truth with revelation as it interprets Scripture for the body.		

The Source and Structure of Truth

The Justification of Truth

The question of the nature of truth, which we have considered, differs somewhat from the question of the justification of beliefs and knowledge. Epistemology bears on the first question, "what is truth?" But it also bears on the question of proving beliefs and knowledge, or providing rational, evidential, or experiential evidence that what I believe or the knowledge that I possess is, in fact, true belief and thus true knowledge of God and the world.

Two major approaches to the question of the justification of belief/knowledge are foundationalism and nonfoundationalism or coherentism.

Foundationalism

The foundationalist perspective holds "that some beliefs, basic or foundational beliefs, are justified apart from their relations to other beliefs, while all other beliefs derive their justification from that of foundational beliefs."[47] Knowledge, and justification of one's beliefs and perceptions, has a "two-tier structure."[48] The lower structure is the foundational one, in which beliefs, perceptions, and knowledge do not need to be justified by their relation to some other, more basic belief. They are self-justified, or self-evident, or "properly basic" beliefs or items of knowledge.

The second tier of beliefs, knowledge, and perceptions are justified in relation to the foundational beliefs from which they are inferred or deduced to be true. These beliefs and items of knowledge are not self-evidently true, nor are they properly basic. Rather they depend on the truth value of more fundamental beliefs. The foundationalist philosopher will pay heed to causes and effects in relation to the knowledge and beliefs that are deemed to be true. A specific belief or item of knowledge one holds might not be properly basic or foundational, which would mean that the justification for believing it could be easily overturned should a more foundational belief be appropriated that shows the other belief to be false. One might, for example, be fully convinced that he or she has seen a ghost. However, that belief would be overturned when the perceiver discovers that the "ghost" was really a jokester wearing a white sheet, or that the ghost was part of a dream. That the perceiver has seen a ghost is an inference based on a limited perception in a specific moment of time. That belief is in no way *foundational*, however, and should be held tentatively.

René Descartes is considered by many to be the father of classic, modern foundationalism. He sought to ground all knowledge on a single, indubitable, unassailable truth that needed no external verification or basis upon anything else. For Descartes, that truth was *Cogito ergo sum*, "I think therefore I am." As a thinking being, Descartes believed he must also be an existing being. All other knowledge and true beliefs, including his belief in the existence of God, would be derived from that unassailable foundation.

Classic foundationalism, in its ancient and modern forms,[49] holds that once the foundational belief is established, beliefs can be determined to be true knowledge or false only in reference to and as a logical derivation of that true foundation. According to the classic perspective,

Nonfoundationalism (Coherentism)

Whereas the noetic structure of foundationalism, as a school of epistemological justification, has been described metaphorically as a building (often a pyramid) with first-order and second-order tiers of beliefs stacked upon each other, nonfoundationalism (or coherentism) has often been depicted as a "web" of beliefs (or sometimes as a log raft), with no one particular belief holding a higher or more fundamental epistemological status than any other. The beliefs that comprise one's particular web (one could hold simultaneously to any number of different belief systems or webs at a given time, assuming they are not fatally contradictory) all hang together and are mutually dependent on each other for their veracity and justification as true knowledge. Within a web, or matrix, or system of belief or knowledge, there is a causal relation between each item. They are connected to each other, making up a paradigm, but it is difficult to explain the relation in terms of specific causality. There are no indubitable, noninferential beliefs that support that entire system. Rather, each supports the other with little attention to hierarchy.

Nonfoundationalism, or coherentism, appeals less to those who desire a logically, rationally, or scientifically rigorous certainty for the justification of their beliefs and more to those who see belief and the structure of its justification to be more dynamic, organic, interconnected, and holistic. Nonfoundationalists also focus on the reality and importance of community in the process of forming beliefs and justifying knowledge. Similarly, nonfoundationalism appeals to those who prefer the paradoxical, mystical, and less rational, scientific and cognitive aspects of theology. Nonfoundationalists often focus on "faith" in the theological process as itself a way of knowing. Sometimes, though not always, coherentists are less concerned with whether specific beliefs can be shown to correspond with actual *facts* of the external, or *real* world, and more concerned with whether one is able to arrive at an internally satisfactory account of life, belief, meaning, truth, and knowledge. It is important to recognize, however, that nonfoundationalists are not necessarily nonrealists when it comes to the question of the nature of truth. Nonfoundationalism, we recall, is a category of the *justification* of truth and knowledge, not a category of the *nature* of truth and knowledge. Thus, nonfoundationalists or coherentists explore how entire systems, webs, or paradigms of knowledge can be justified as a whole.

The Justification of Truth

Foundationalism	Nonfoundationalism (Coherentism)
foundational knowledge, once established, cannot be questioned because it is certain and indubitable. The key question, of course, is whether the foundation has been correctly established. On this view, then, one must be sure that the foundational belief is indubitable and unassailable. For classic foundationalists, the only beliefs considered potentially foundational relate to reason or experience—beliefs that can be publically verified and held up unfailingly to scientific and rational scrutiny.[50] Moderate forms of foundationalism have also emerged, some in reaction to the stronger version of Descartes. These allow for foundational beliefs other than those of reason and experience.[51] Moderate foundationalists also seek a more modest kind of justification of knowledge and belief. These forms of foundationalism have been prefaced by adjectives such as "moderate," "soft," and "modest." They recognize that, for something to be deemed true, it must bear some public relation to an already established truth or recognized authority. Unlike classic foundationalists, however, moderate (or weak) foundationalists hold that a foundational or noninferential belief can be justified by simply having *good reason* to believe it and a lack of reason to disbelieve it. Modest foundationalism "implies that foundational beliefs need not possess or yield certainty, and need not deductively support justified nonfoundational beliefs."[52] Some theologians have suggested that the Bible is the foundation for all theological knowledge. For a proposition or belief that relates to, or is derived from, the content of the Bible to be deemed true, and thus justified, knowledge, one must show it to be true in relation to the already assumed truth of the Bible's veracity, trustworthiness, etc. That other truth, then, could not be considered true if it were not based upon the foundation of Scripture's authority, or inerrancy. Thus, the truth of Scripture (the doctrine of its nature) is logically prior to other truths, such as God's existence, His covenant faithfulness, and so forth. Yet other theologians might make God's existence the foundation of all knowledge, so that one's doctrine of Scripture derives from and rests upon the more certain knowledge of God's existence and faithfulness.	Postmodern theology is often more attuned to the concern for coherence than it is for establishing knowledge on indubitable, certain foundations. This is because postmodernism emphasizes the historical, cultural, and linguistic situatedness of knowledge. We are historical creatures, products of a time and situation that is distinct from every other. Thus the only way we can even hope to acquire justification is via appeal to criterion that are specific to our own situations, cultures, languages, experiences, and so on. Thus, truth can only be verified in relation to a given, local, individualistic situation. In this postmodern context, some theologians have proposed a "postfoundationalist" way of doing theology. These theologians have pointed out the demise of the stronger, more radical forms of Enlightenment foundationalism and have recognized many of the insights of postmodern thought (such as the linguistic, social, cultural, and historical embeddedness of thought, knowledge, and belief). They argue that rationality is not always a "responsible choice" of the knower. Rather, knowers have received a tradition, a language, a structure of rationality from which it is not always possible to escape. We are thrown into a world and many of our ideas and thoughts are given to us by virtue of being in that world. We do not always begin the reasoning process from logical, first principles from which we can then deduce second and third principles that are justified on indubitable foundations. Rather, we begin *from within* a web of belief—a context. J. Wentzel van Huyssteen, proposing a postfoundationalist theology, distinguishes his approach from both the foundationalist and the nonfoundationalist (which he points out often degenerates into radical relativism). Postfoundationalism, he says, recognizes contextuality and yet wishes to "point creatively beyond the confines of the local community, group, or culture towards a plausible form of interdisciplinary conversation."[53] Postfoundationalism, van Huyssteen states, is an alternative epistemological option that is concerned "to identify the shared resources of human rationality in different modes of reflection, and then to reach beyond the walls of our own epistemic communities in cross-contextual, cross-cultural, and cross-disciplinary conversation."[54] Some coherentist views of justification are compatible with a realist view of truth. The realist view simply states that what one knows is true reality—there is a reality outside of our perceptions of it, even though our perceptions are limited. A coherentist view of justification can align with a realist view of truth because for some, coherence may be the only hope of epistemic verification, but *what* is actually being shown to be true is objectively and ontologically (and/or metaphysically) *real*.

53. J. Wentzel van Huyssteen, *Essays in Postfoundationalist Theology* (Grand Rapids: Eerdmans, 1997), 4.
54. Ibid.

47. M. R. D., "Coherentism," in *Cambridge Dictionary of Philosophy*, 154.
48. L. B., "Foundationalism," in *Cambridge Dictionary of Philosophy*, 321.
49. Ancient classic foundationalism is represented by Aristotle and Thomas Aquinas, whereas modern classic foundationalism is represented by Descartes. See J. P. Moreland and William Lane Craig, *Philosophical Foundations for a Christian Worldview* (Downers Grove, IL: InterVarsity Press, 2003), 113ff.
50. Ibid, 112.
51. Cf. the work of Alvin Plantinga for his version of foundationalism, Reformed epistemology. See e.g., Plantinga's contribution to *Religious Experience and Religious Belief: Essays in the Epistemology of Religion*, ed. Joseph Runzo and Craig Ihara (Lanham, MD: University Press of America, 1986).
52. Moser, Mulder, and Trout, *The Theory of Knowledge*, 87–88.

PART TEN

The Relationship Between the Testaments

The Relationship Between the Testaments and Its Implication for Theology

One of the most significant hermeneutical issues for Christian theologians is the relationship between the Old Testament and the New Testament. As N. H. Ridderbos said of the Old Testament–New Testament connection as central to theological discussion, "that is just about the whole story; the whole of theology is involved in that."[1] The Bible is the primary sourcebook for Christian theology, and it is generally considered to be a unified body of literature as Christian *canon,* but it is also characterized by diversity in its theology, history, and literature genres. This has led some theologians, particularly in the field of biblical theology, to work exclusively in the Old Testament or in the New Testament. Some have inferred from this conclusion that the Testaments represent two incompatible or completely unrelated theologies. The Reformation hermeneutical principle of "Scripture interprets Scripture," however, was meant to include the whole Bible.[2] Thus the most helpful kinds of biblical theology treat both Testaments as aspects contributing to the whole. Each is significant in its own right and that significance intensifies as it is viewed in terms of the completed biblical canon.

The Old Testament gives the story of creation, fall, restoration, election (of Israel), and redemption of the world through God's special relationship to Israel. Other complementary themes include covenant, the law, the words of the prophets, and the laments and praises of the psalmists. The New Testament unveils Jesus Christ's life and work in the Gospels and moves to the story of the church's emergence. Much teaching about the implications of the way of the Christian comes through the Epistles. The apocalyptic and eschatological vision of the eternal kingdom of God is viewed in Revelation. The relationship between the Testaments finds its hinge in the story of Jesus Christ incarnate in the Gospels. In Christ the hope and faith expressed so often by the Old Testament prophets and saints finds its ultimate fulfillment. And in Christ the hope and faith of the New Testament saints finds its foundation.

Christian theologians of various orientations would hold the entire Bible to be divinely inspired and thus authoritative for faith and practice. However, theologians may *approach* the Testaments very differently, depending on how they understand the content and form of the Testaments to be related. John Feinberg has provided a helpful way to delineate the relationship between the Testaments, and the thematic and theological content of which they speak, as one of *continuity and discontinuity.*[3] We will modify this model somewhat, using the key words *distinction* and *similarity.* We will focus on the larger issue of the unity and the diversity of the Testaments within theology, but we will also be looking at the extent to which theologians perceive distinctions and similarities between the Testaments, in relation to such topics as law and grace, the issue of salvation, and the nature of the church.

Most evangelical and many Christian theologians hold to the essential unity of the Testaments as parts of one Christian Bible. However, when practicing interpretation and theology, it is possible to see elements of divergence between the Testaments, while retaining a basic belief in their essential unity as a completed canon, with each Testament equally inspired by God.

Subsequently we will present a variety of views on the relationship between the Testaments in relation to the task of constructing a biblical theology. Thus the first discussion lies mainly in the realm of systematic/ doctrinal theology, while the latter debate remains a most significant issue for biblical theology.

---

1. Cited in Henning Graf Reventlow, *Problems of Biblical Theology in the Twentieth Century* (Philadelphia: Fortress, 1986), 11.
2. Graeme Goldsworthy, "Relationship of Old Testament and New Testament," in *New Dictionary of Biblical Theology* (Downers Grove, IL: InterVarsity Press, 2000), 81.
3. John S. Feinberg, ed., *Continuity and Discontinuity: Perspectives on the Relationship Between the Old and New Testaments* (Westchester, IL: Crossway, 1988). See also David L. Baker, *Two Testaments, One Bible: A Study of the Theological Relationship Between the Old and New Testaments,* 2d ed. (Downers Grove, IL: InterVarsity Press, 1991).

The Relationship Between the Testaments

Unity or Diversity? A Question for Systematic/Doctrinal Theology

Unity, Emphasizing Continuity	Unity, Emphasizing Both Continuity and Discontinuity	Classic and Revised Dispensationalism: Unity, Emphasizing Discontinuity	Progressive Dispensationalism: Unity, with Continuity and Discontinuity	Diversity and Plurality
John Calvin	Martin Luther	Charles Ryrie, John Walvoord	Craig Blaising, Darrel Bock	Rudolf Bultmann
Reformer John Calvin devoted significant space in *Institutes of the Christian Religion* to the similarities—and to the differences—between the Testaments. He focused on the similarities of the Testaments in terms of their ultimate objective, which is to serve as God's special revelation, through which people come to saving faith and knowledge of God in Christ. In book 2, chapter 9, he further explains that "Christ, although he was known to the Jews under the law, was at length clearly revealed only in the gospel." Calvin sees a clear progression in the history of redemption in which humanity is given something (hope in Christ) that enables them to enter into covenant with God. The nature of this hope is not fully understood, however, until Christ comes to earth. Calvin writes: "For when he appeared in this, his image, he, as it were, made himself visible;	Martin Luther, explaining justification by faith alone, writes that the Scriptures are divided in two parts: "commandments and promises."[14] The commandments, Luther asserts, "show us what we ought to do but do not give us the power to do it; they are intended to teach man to know himself, that through them he may recognize his inability to do good and may despair of his own ability."[15] Luther saw the Old Testament's teaching of law as having the function of bringing people to faith in the gospel out of a personal realization of inability to be righteous. A command such as "you shall not covet," he says, has, in effect, the function of causing a person to despair: "Therefore, in order not to covet, and to fulfill the command, a man is compelled to despair of himself, and to seek elsewhere and from some one else the help which he does not find in himself. . . . And as we fare with this one command, so we fare with all; for it is equally impossible for us to keep any one of them."[16] Luther says that to fulfill the	Classic dispensational theology is typically very concerned with the question of the relationship between the Testaments. Dispensationalists see the Bible as an essential, theological unity that expresses within it a diversity of ways in which God has worked in redemptive history. The name *dispensational* signifies a characteristic emphasis on marked distinctions between the various and successive stages of redemptive history as they unfold in Scripture. Charles Ryrie defines dispensationalism as "a distinguishable economy in the outworking of God's program."[25] According to dispensationalism, God works out His redemptive plan according to various "economies," much like the management of a household;[26] man is responsible to respond in each dispensation according to the level of revelation God provides. The introduction to the revised 1967 edition of the *Scofield Reference Bible* explains that the dispensations "are distinguished, exhibiting the progressive order of God's dealings with humanity, the increasing	Progressive dispensationalists have also taken the Bible to be an essential unity, but have discerned, like classic and revised dispensationalists, strong elements of diversity and discontinuity between the Testaments. Progressive dispensationalists distinguished themselves by an explicit attempt to focus more on the *literary* dimensions of the biblical text than have classic and revised dispensationalists. Craig Blaising writes, "It should be noted that progressive dispensationalism is not an abandonment of 'literal' interpretation for spiritual interpretation. Progressive dispensationalism is a development of 'literal' interpretation into a more consistent historical-literary interpretation."[30] Progressive dispensationalists see the relation between the Testaments and the plan of God that unfolds within its canonical story line as a "progression." The New Testament does not take meaning away from the Old Testament, but complements the Old Testament's meaning, providing new insights and new aspects of God's revelation	For Rudolf Bultmann, the Bible's diversity and plurality cannot and should not be overcome by a dogmatic or theological appeal to divine revelation, with its usual emphasis on Scripture's uniformity and essential unity. Bultmann does not see the theological content of revelation as being straightforwardly contained in the biblical witness of the Old and New Testaments, waiting simply to be extricated by the interpreter through "objective" methodological approaches. Bultmann was an influential "form critic" of the New Testament. Form criticism was the interpretive process in which segments of text were examined by a historical and literary eye to determine their "genre" (literary form). The form of the literature then helps the reader to determine the historical, social, and cultural situation of the authors of the text. This will help the reader determine the meaning of the text. Bultmann interpreted the New Testament with reference to two spheres of history: the history of the actual events described by the

The Relationship Between the Testaments

Unity or Diversity? A Question for Systematic/Doctrinal Theology

Unity, Emphasizing Continuity	Unity, Emphasizing Both Continuity and Discontinuity	Classic and Revised Dispensationalism: Unity, Emphasizing Discontinuity	Progressive Dispensationalism: Unity, with Continuity and Discontinuity	Diversity and Plurality
Calvin	Luther	Ryrie, Walvoord	Blaising, Bock	Bultmann
whereas his appearance had before been indistinct and shadowed."[4] In speaking of the relationship between law and gospel, Calvin writes that the gospel "did not so supplant the entire law as to bring forward a different way of salvation. Rather, the gospel confirmed and satisfied whatever the law had promised, and gave substance to the shadows."[5] Thus, there is a distinction between the law and the gospel, but one must be careful not to exaggerate the difference. The *way* of salvation was always the same, but the subjective *knowledge* given to the saved as to how they were being saved, and as to what object their hope actually pointed toward, differed, as shadows from substance. In the opening sentence of his chapter on the similarity of the Old and New Testaments, Calvin writes, "Now we can clearly see from what has already been said that all men adopted by God into the company of his people since the beginning of the world were covenanted to him by the same law and by the bond of the	commands given in the Old Testament, one must come to the Christ of the New Testament: "Thus the promises of God give what the commandments of God demand and fulfill what the law prescribes so that all things may be God's alone, both the commandments and the fulfilling of the commandments. . . . Therefore the promises of God belong to the New Testament, nay, they are the New Testament."[17] The source and ground of salvation was considered by Luther to be the same for Old Testament saints as for the New. They had "the same faith and Gospel as we have."[18] The only difference, Luther explains, is "they believed in the coming and promised Seed; we believe in the Seed that is come and has been given. But it is all the one truth of the promise, and hence also one faith, one Spirit, one Christ, one Lord, now as then, and forever."[19] If there is continuity in regard to the ground and source of salvation, what then is the nature of the discontinuity between the	purpose which runs through and links together time-periods during which man has been responsible for specific and varying tests as to his obedience to God, from the beginning of history to its end. . . . As a further aid to comprehending the divine economy of the ages, a recognition of the dispensations is of highest value, so long as it is clearly understood that throughout all the Scriptures there is only one basis of salvation, i.e., by grace through faith; and that strict limits cannot be placed upon the terminations of the dispensations because (1) there is some overlapping, and (2) the divinely given stewardship may continue after the time-era of special testing has ended."[27] While all dispensationalists see at least three clear "economies" in the Bible, many hold to seven, and some see ten or more. Dispensationalists also distinguish between various covenants in the biblical revelation (Adamic—pre and post-fall, Noahaic, Abrahamic, Davidic). Craig Blaising and Darrel Bock	as it unfolds in history. As Darrel Bock writes, "A complementary emphasis does not remove meaning; it makes new, sometimes fresh, additional connections. . . ."[31] Bock contends that the progressive dispensational hermeneutic differs from traditional dispensationalism in that it does not merely "repeat" Old Testament themes in the New Testament era without allowing those themes (e.g., "Israel") to be given extended meanings. It also, he says, differs from covenantal hermeneutics in that it does not just substitute an Old Testament concept or theme for a New Testament replacement (the "church" for "Israel").[32] Bock, defending progressive dispensationalism from charges that it neglects the traditional view of stable meaning in hermeneutics, writes about the relationship between the Testaments in interpretation. "When progressives speak of a complementary relationship between Old and New Testament texts, they are claiming	written documents (e.g., the life of the Jesus as described by the evangelists) and the history of the composition of the texts themselves (the writings of the evangelists, witnesses, and followers). We have no direct access to the former kind of history. We cannot go back in time to observe the original Jesus. Therefore, we must be concerned only with the latter history, what amounts to the history of religious experiences by those who claim to have known Him.[39] For Bultmann, it is this experience that modern people can seek to emulate through an existential encounter with God in Christ. Thus Bultmann's concern was finding and proclaiming the *kerygma*, the central idea of the gospel, after having stripped it of its supernatural, "mythical" garb. For Bultmann, revelation is a dialectical encounter in which God meets the human being through the event of a disclosure. Revelation is "that opening up of what is hidden which is absolutely necessary and decisive for man if he is to achieve

The Relationship Between the Testaments

Unity or Diversity? A Question for Systematic/Doctrinal Theology

Unity, Emphasizing Continuity	Unity, Emphasizing Both Continuity and Discontinuity	Classic and Revised Dispensationalism: Unity, Emphasizing Discontinuity	Progressive Dispensationalism: Unity, with Continuity and Discontinuity	Diversity and Plurality
Calvin	Luther	Ryrie, Walvoord	Blaising, Bock	Bultmann
same doctrine as obtains among us."[6] Calvin is arguing against the claims of "Servetus and certain madmen of the Anabaptist sect," who, according to Calvin wrote disparagingly of the Israelites, their place in the history of redemption, and the place of the law as a means of dispensing grace. They saw only a negative purpose for the law, as being dramatically distinct from the grace of the new covenant. For Calvin, the covenant made with the Old Testament saints and the covenant made with New Testament saints differs only in terms of "the mode of dispensation,"[7] that is, the manner and degree to which God revealed the substance of their faith to the faithful ones. For Calvin, the Old Testament saints "had Christ as pledge of their covenant" and "put in him all trust of future blessedness." This means that, in the theologies of old and new, the orientation is toward the knowledge of God in Christ and to the promise of spiritual and eternal life.[8] In a subsequent chapter on the "differences between the two testaments," Calvin discusses them	Testaments? For Luther, it lies largely in the nature and role of the law as compared to that of the gospel: "But the subsequent giving of the law to the Jews is not on a par with this promise. The law was given in order that by its light they might the better come to know their cursed state and the more fervently and heartily desire the promised Seed; wherein they had an advantage over all the heathen world. But they turned this advantage into a disadvantage; they undertook to keep the law by their own strength, and failed to learn from it their needy and cursed state."[20] The law was given, Luther explains, to cause those who attempted to follow it to turn in despair to God, "to know their accursed nature and learn to call upon Christ."[21] Lest one think that Luther holds to a negative view of the Old Testament and of the law it contains, i.e., *merely* as a way to drive men to despair to turn to the positive solution in the Gospel, Luther offers, in his *Introduction to the Old Testament*,	have delineated differences between three versions of dispensationalism: classical, revised, and progressive.[28] Classical dispensationalism (e.g., C. I. Scofield) features a distinction between God's salvific purposes as having both an earthly purpose and a heavenly purpose. In His earthly purpose, God will re-create the physical world and preserve an earthly people who will dwell on it for eternity—even eternity beyond the millennium (the literal thousand years of peace). But God is also redeeming a heavenly, spiritual people (all the redeemed of all the ages *before* that generation to which Christ appears on the earth. This latter group will comprise the earthly, eternal people, those who are converted to Christ at His appearing, and these will exist forever on the earth). Both classical and revised dispensationalists uphold some kind of distinction between Israel and the church, being two very different entities with two different purposes in God's redemptive plan. The future for Israel is, in some way,	that a normal, contextually determined reading often brings concepts from the Holy Scriptures together in the New Testament in a way that completes and expounds what was already present in the older portion of God's Word. As revelation proceeds, the texts themselves, New and Old Testament, are brought together in a way that links concepts together, so that both old and fresh associations are made (Matt. 13:52)."[33] This way of interpreting the Bible canonically and integratively, Bock contends, still enables a "stable meaning" of the text, because the meaning "emerges from within a normal reading of the text." The only difference, Bock maintains, between traditional and progressive readings, then, "is that progressives are asking dispensationalists to work more integratively with the biblical text."[34] Progressive dispensationalists, according to Blaising and Bock, "understand the dispensations not simply as *different* arrangements between God and humankind, but as	'salvation' or 'authenticity'; i.e., revelation here is the disclosure of God to man—whether this disclosure is thought to take place through the communication of knowledge, through a mediating doctrine about God, or whether it is an occurrence that puts man in a new situation."[40] For Bultmann, then, the form and content of Scripture, when the *kerygma* is extracted from it, provide a possibility for the reader to encounter God in the act of existential faith. It makes sense, then, that the diversity and plurality exhibited by the Scriptures stand out over any formal or material unity that could be discerned. The "kerygma" is presented through Scripture in a plurality of ways through a plurality of events. Bultmann explicitly rejects Oscar Cullman's salvation-historical approach of "carrying up the statements of the various New Testament writings to the same level" as leading to an "illicit harmonization." For Bultmann, the history of salvation is not an idea with which the New Testament

The Relationship Between the Testaments

Unity or Diversity? A Question for Systematic/Doctrinal Theology

Unity, Emphasizing Continuity	Unity, Emphasizing Both Continuity and Discontinuity	Classic and Revised Dispensationalism: Unity, Emphasizing Discontinuity	Progressive Dispensationalism: Unity, with Continuity and Discontinuity	Diversity and Plurality
Calvin	Luther	Ryrie, Walvoord	Blaising, Bock	Bultmann
under four main headings: (1) In the Old Testament, the stress is on earthly benefits, "which, however, were to lead to heavenly concerns."[9] (2) The Old Testament presents spiritual and ultimate truth by typologies ("images and ceremonies typifying Christ").[10] (3) In the Old Testament, God's Word is given in the letter (thus, "literal") whereas in the New Testament it is given on the heart (thus, "spiritual").[11] (4) The Old Testament is "bondage," because it produces "fear in men's minds," whereas the New Testament is "freedom," because "it lifts them to trust and assurance." Thus, Calvin presents both the similarities and differences as he viewed them between the Old and the New Testaments. As he stated, "I freely admit the differences in Scripture, to which attention is called, but in such a way as not to detract from its established unity."[12] Both unity and diversity, similarities and distinctions, should be affirmed. One must interpret it theologically, in light of the realization of the progression	this commendation of the merits of the Old Testament as the Word of God to be interpreted literally and with great benefit. He writes, against those who have a "little opinion" of the Old Testament, that because the New Testament is based on the Old Testament, and the preaching of Christ fulfills the "sayings of the Old Testament," it is "not to be despised, but diligently read."[22] Nonetheless, the Old Testament is "a book of laws, which teaches what men are to do and not to do," while "the New Testament is a Gospel or book of grace, and teaches where one is to get the power to fulfill the law."[23] While these basic distinctions hold, Luther sees the New Testament also contains "laws and commandments for the ruling of the flesh," and the Old Testament provides "certain promises and offers of grace, by which the holy fathers and prophets, under the law, were kept, like us, under the faith of Christ."[24]	different from the future of the church, as it is grounded in a physical and political reality rather than primarily in the spiritual realm. Dispensationalists find differences between the biblical Testaments, because they see distinctions throughout the unfolding of God's progressive revelation. However, as Ryrie notes, "The concept of progressive revelation does not negate the unity of the Bible but recognizes the diversity of God's unfolding revelation as essential to the unity of his completed revelation."[29] Thus to focus only on the distinctions in the dispensational hermeneutic can be misleading, because in some areas of theological discourse, dispensationalists will find more elements of similarity than will a nondispensational theologian. For example, dispensationalists often claim that they are better able to hold to a consistency, or *continuity*, of word meaning and usage between the Old Testament and the New Testament. The word Israel, they would claim, means the same	*successive* arrangements in the *progressive* revelation and accomplishment of redemption." The plan of redemption, they say, "has different aspects to it . . . but all these dispensations point to a future culmination in which God will *both* politically administer Israel *and* indwell all of them equally (without ethnic distinctions) by the Holy Spirit. Consequently, the dispensations *progress* by revealing different aspects of the final unified redemption."[35] Contrary to classic and revised dispensationalists who viewed the church as being in a separate category in God's redemptive plan (what some called a "parenthesis, or others an "intercalation"), the church, for progressive dispensationalists, is a "new manifestation of grace, a new dispensation in the history of redemption."[36] Progressive dispensationalists view the covenants (not just the new covenant, but the Abrahamic and Davidic) as having been, and being progressively—though only partially—fulfilled in the present age, looking "forward to	authors are greatly concerned: "In any case, it is a gross overstatement to say that the entire New Testament presupposes a unified conception of the history of salvation, and the oldest formulations of faith do not seem to me to provide proof of this."[41] If there exists no essential unity, but rather a remarkable diversity and plurality of theological and historical expression in the New Testament, how much more would he see the diversity and plurality between the New Testament and the Old Testament. For Bultmann the Old Testament is beneficial for the Christian theologian when interpreted in existential categories, but is not to be seen as an essential supplement to the New Testament kerygma. Most higher critics of the Bible, whether their specialty was New Testament or Old Testament, tended to read the Bible less as a unity than as composite fragments of literature and history. While Bultmann shows this influence in his sensitivity to the diversity of the New Testament

The Relationship Between the Testaments

Unity or Diversity? A Question for Systematic/Doctrinal Theology

Unity, Emphasizing Continuity	Unity, Emphasizing Both Continuity and Discontinuity	Classic and Revised Dispensationalism: Unity, Emphasizing Discontinuity	Progressive Dispensationalism: Unity, with Continuity and Discontinuity	Diversity and Plurality
Calvin	Luther	Ryrie, Walvoord	Blaising, Bock	Bultmann

Diversity and Plurality (Bultmann):

presentation, he at least tried to provide a theological unity to Scripture through the emphasis on a *kerygma* that can be presently and existentially appropriated.

James Barr is a contemporary example of a biblical scholar who emphasizes the diversity present in the biblical text. He holds that the Bible's theology is most accurately represented when its diversity is adequately recognized. He warns against the tendency to subsume Scripture's diversity under a theologically motivated emphasis on canonical unity.

39. Cf. Gerald Bray, *Biblical Interpretation: Past and Present* (Downers Grove, IL: InterVarsity Press, 1996), 438–39.
40. Rudolf Bultmann, *Existence and Faith* (London: Hodder & Stoughton, 1961), 59.
41. Ibid., 235.

Progressive Dispensationalism (Blaising, Bock):

complete fulfillment at the return of Christ."[37] Finally, regarding the important notion of the "kingdom of God," progressive dispensationalists see one promised eschatological kingdom which has both spiritual and political dimensions. . . . The progressive revelation of one or another aspect of the eschatological kingdom (whether spiritual or political) prior to the eternal reign of Christ, follows the history of Jesus Christ and is dependent on Him as He acts according to the will of the Father."[38]

30. Blaising and Bock, *Progressive Dispensationalism.*
31. Herbert W. Bateman IV, ed., *Three Central Issues in Contemporary Dispensationalism: A Comparison of Traditional and Progressive Views* (Grand Rapids: Kregel, 1999), 90.
32. Ibid.
33. Ibid., 89.
34. Ibid.
35. Ibid., 48.
36. Ibid., 49.
37. Ibid., 53.
38. Ibid., 54.

Classic and Revised Dispensationalism (Ryrie, Walvoord):

thing (or things) in the Old Testament as in the New when it refers to the earthly, national people of God; thus the prophecies of the Old regarding the glorious, eternal future for national, political Israel must be awaiting their earthly (national-political) fulfillment in a future dispensation.

25. Charles Ryrie, "Dispensationalism," in *Evangelical Dictionary of Theology*, ed. Walter A. Elwell (Grand Rapids: Baker, 1984), 322.
26. Ibid.
27. *The New Scofield Reference Bible* (New York: Oxford University Press, 1967), vii.
28. Craig A. Blaising and Darrell L. Bock, *Progressive Dispensationalism* (Wheaton, IL: Bridgepoint, 1993), 52.
29. Ryrie, "Dispensationalism," in *Evangelical Dictionary of Theology,* 322.

Unity, Emphasizing Both Continuity and Discontinuity (Luther):

14. Martin Luther, "A Treatise on Christian Liberty," cited in *Martin Luther's Basic Theological Writings*, ed. Timothy F. Lull (Minneapolis: Fortress, 1989), 600. Also cited in Hugh Thomson Kerr, *A Compend of Luther's Theology* (Philadelphia: Westminster, 1966), 6.
15. Ibid.
16. Ibid., 600–601.
17. Ibid., 601.
18. Martin Luther, "The Magnificat," *Works of Martin Luther*, 6 vols. (Philadelphia: Muhlenberg, 1915–43), 3:196.
19. Ibid.
20. Ibid., 196–97.
21. Ibid., 7.
22. Martin Luther, *Prefaces to the Old Testament: Martin Luther's Basic Theological Writings*, ed. Timothy F. Lull (Minneapolis: Fortress, 1989), 118.
23. Ibid., 119.
24. Ibid., 120.

Unity, Emphasizing Continuity (Calvin):

of redemption in human history and the progressive unfolding of divine revelation, from the first until now.

For Calvin, the reality of the progress of redemption, accompanied by a progress in revelation, meant that the New Testament was accorded a kind of priority over the Old Testament.[13] Calvin's emphasis on the similarities between the Testaments in this respect finds its legacy in much of Reformed, or covenantal, interpretation of Scripture.

4. John Calvin, *Institutes of the Christian Religion*, 2 vols. ed. John T. McNeill, trans. Ford Lewis Battles (Philadelphia: Westminster, 1960), 2:9.
5. Ibid.
6. Ibid., 2:10.
7. Ibid.
8. Ibid.
9. Ibid.
10. Ibid.
11. Ibid.
12. Ibid.
13. Feinberg, *Continuity and Discontinuity*, 73.

Interpretive Issues with Respect to the Relationship Between the Testaments for Biblical Theology

METHODOLOGICAL EXCLUSIVITY VERSUS METHODOLOGICAL INCLUSIVITY

A debate has raged in the field of biblical theology regarding the feasibility and propriety of what James Barr has called a pan-biblical theological method. Is it possible, even if it is desirable, to appeal to the data of the New Testament in order to shed light on the theology of the Old Testament, and vice versa? Two basic positions can be discerned on the issue in the field of biblical theology. In some respects, the issue revolves around differing views regarding whether biblical theology should strive to be a prescriptive or a normative field. If prescriptive, then theological formulations attempt, with the backing of biblical, canonical, or traditional authority, to *prescribe* how one should live and what one ought to believe. If normative, biblical theology should merely attempt to *describe* the theological understandings and developments within a particular religious culture and historical situation, the nation of Israel in the Old Testament or the first-century church in the New Testament. However, many proponents who uphold description as central still believe that we cannot entirely escape the realm of prescription when describing theological understanding. Similarly, proponents of the emphasis on prescription expend tremendous energy on the work of description, often employing the rigorous, descriptive work of historical-critical methods. It is probably more accurate to describe the difference as being that of methodological inclusivity versus methodological exclusivity.

Methodological inclusivity holds that, in order to truly understand the Old Testament, one must also look at the New Testament, and vice versa. Exclusivity holds that using the New Testament to understand the Old Testament will only be an obstacle in coming to an adequate and objective understanding of the text in its historical setting.

Subjective Theologies		Both/And Approaches	
Methodological Inclusivity Bervard Childs	Methodological Exclusivity James Barr	John Goldingay The Testaments as Parallel, Joint Witness to God	Gerhard Maier Salvation-Historical Approach: Unity with Diversity

Bervard Childs holds that, in order to fully understand the Old Testament as Christian Scripture, one must also seek to understand the New Testament as Christian Scripture. Both have been accorded canonical status by the believing church, so in order to read Scripture *as* Scripture, and to understand it as it was understood as authoritative canon, the theologian must read it as such. At the same time, the exegete should not neglect the insights of historical-critical thought and related insights of canon criticism.

Childs's canonical approach, as one writer explains, reflects dissatisfaction with form, source, and redaction criticism. Childs thought that the usual historical-critical approach segregated some aspects of the text from others and grounded interpretation solely in historical considerations and not in canon. Canonical considerations are actually reflected in the finished product of the text as a complete literary unit.[42] Edgar McKnight writes, "Bervard Childs is less concerned with discovering the hermeneutical principles used in the process of canonization than in analyzing the final form of the Biblical books."[43] And, "To take the canonical shape of these texts seriously is to seek to do justice to a literature which Israel transmitted as a record of God's revelation to his people along with Israel's response."[44]

James Barr, in describing the character of biblical theology as distinct from that of doctrinal or dogmatic theology, doubts the possibility of what he calls a "pan-biblical theology," that purports to construct a unified theology which appeals both to the Old and New Testaments.[48] He is unconvinced by the canonical approach of Brevard Childs and its emphasis on the essential unity of Scripture as providing the data for theology. Barr works from the foundation of the distinction made by J. P. Gabler between doctrinal theology and biblical theology, with the former being authoritative and prescriptive, while the latter is descriptive, seeking to present the theology *of* the Bible, and of particular books and biblical authors.[49]

Barr emphasizes the differences between the theologies of the Old and the New Testaments. He states, "When taken as wholes—which is the stated purpose of most biblical theologies in general—they are not congruent, nor even closely analogical. There are a multitude of connections, similarities and relationships, which many scholars have been engaged in tracking down. But the synthetic, holistic shape of the one is very different from the other."[50] Barr, as a Christian, recognizes that the Old and New Testaments belong together as essential parts of the whole, the Bible. He is concerned, however, that, given

Old Testament theologian John Goldingay offers a mediating position between the historical (diachronic) and canonical (synchronic) approaches to the relationship between the Testaments in the context of biblical theology. He states, "If OT and NT are in fact one in faith, and the coming of Jesus is the climax of the purpose Yahweh was concerned with in OT times, it will not be unscientific to allow this link between the two testaments to affect the way one presents the OT material. Indeed, this may enable one to see what someone else might miss."[52] Goldingay is careful to note that the distinctions between Old Testament and New Testament themes and emphases "means that a Christian's investigation of OT theology may be in danger of underplaying distinctive OT themes such as the law, Israel, the land, and worship."[53] Thus, there is a self-contained nature to the Old Testament that legitimizes a purely *Old Testament* theology.

Goldingay suggests that a "parallel status" be given to both, "as joint witnesses to the one God whose speaking in each helps us to understand the Christ who came between the testaments. The Old lays the theological foundation for the New and sometimes explicitly looks forward in a hope which the Christian sees confirmed or fulfilled in Christ. The New presupposes this foundation and

The salvation-historical interpretive school, famously propounded in the twentieth century by such scholars as Oscar Cullmann, has historically found a steady stream of advocates in many eras of theological study, from liberal to conservative camps. The attempt by those who interpret the Bible according to a salvation-historical flow has been to find a strain of unity within the biblical account, whether that unity comprises merely a "history of religions" approach (and thus a methodological secularism) or whether the approach is a dogmatic one, in which the interpreter seeks to make normative statements about God's actions in history as detailed in His revelation (which would accordingly be applicable to the interpreter's contemporary situation).

For the German theologian Gerhard Maier, the unity of the story of redemption by God ultimately realized in Christ can be seen in the composition of the two Testaments as witnesses to God's work in redemption. The salvation-historical approach Maier uses allows for certain "gaps" in the narrative depictions and in the synoptic comparisons: God has simply not seen fit to explain *everything* about His redemptive plan. The historical and literary particulars of the biblical witness allow for discontinuities within the overall unity of the biblical word.

The Relationship Between the Testaments

Subjective Theologies

Methodological Inclusivity	Methodological Exclusivity	Both/And Approaches	
Childs	Barr	Goldingay	Maier
In speaking of Childs's *Introduction to the New Testament*, G. T. Sheppard writes, "This volume also forewarns Christian scholars of the Old Testament that they must engage the critical issues raised by the New Testament if we want to understand how Jewish Scripture belongs to the Christian Bible at all. A discipline of Old Testament studies cannot exist without New Testament studies, any more than Jewish Scripture can be understood adequately apart from some engagement with the rabbinic exegetical tradition and oral Torah."[45] Childs writes in his *Introduction to the Old Testament as Scripture* that the goal of the canonical approach is "to take seriously the significance of the canon as a crucial element in understanding the Hebrew Scriptures, and yet to understand the canon in its true historical and theological dimensions." Childs argues against his critics that the canonical-critical approach is a historical reading of Scripture, rather than an ahistorical one. Rather, he says, the issue at stake is the nature of the Bible's historicity and the search for a historical approach. "The whole point of emphasizing the canon is to stress the historical nature of the biblical witness. . . . The study of the canonical shape of the literature is an attempt to do justice to the nature of Israel's unique history. To take the canon	the significant differences and the exactitude of scholarship and varied knowledge specialties that each Testament requires, the "mode in which they belong together," demands a holistic theology of either one or the other Testament. Again, we must emphasize that Barr's claim for the essential disjunction between the Testaments in the task of biblical theology is not related to the very different task of doctrinal theology. In the arena of doctrinal theology, one can take as a matter of faith[51] that the Testaments are integrally and organically related and demand that each be used as a dialogue partner with and resource for the other to construct a theology of the whole. But this connection cannot be fruitful, Barr claims, in the attempt to do justice to the theology, or theologies, of either one or the other, historically and descriptively understood. 48. James Barr, *The Concept of Biblical Theology* (Minneapolis: Fortress, 1999), 4. 49. This is not to say that Barr has no interest in biblical theology's ability to influence life. Rather, the "reading of the Bible, even when done historically, should and must at once provide perspectives which change our perception of the world and affect our deepest interests and purposes." Rather, the priority should be to understand clearly and adequately what a	looks back to Christ, concentrating on what needs to be said in the light of his coming, but encouraging rather than discouraging us to do this against the background of the OT's broader concerns. Faith in Christ with its background in the NT may provide the pre-understanding for our approach to the OT; but where we find the OT saying something in tension with that pre-understanding, our reaction will be to allow it to broaden the latter, not to accept only what conforms to what we know already. Christ helps us to understand the OT, but the OT helps us to understand Christ."[54] Differences in themes and ideas, which are easily discerned, should be seen as complementary, Goldingay asserts. While the two could be studied in isolation from each other, to do so is questionable when viewed from a theological perspective. The Bible is "the normative context for interpreting any one of its parts." Focusing on one Testament to the neglect of another can lead to imbalance. He concludes, "Christian theology needs a biblical theology, rather than an OT theology which has difficulty in referring to Christ, or a NT theology which omits the NT's normative but unspoken background and context."[55] In order to be rightly understood, Goldingay says, the Old Testament needs the New Testament to fill out the picture. The	But the Bible must be viewed theologically as a unity because God is the divine author, and unity (as opposed to disunity or contradiction) is an aspect of His essential character. Also, the Scriptures themselves testify to their own unity in speaking of the Bible (or at least the Old Testament) as Scripture (Luke 24:44; John 5:39; 7:38; 10:35; Rom. 1:2; 4:3; 1 Cor. 15:3; 1 Tim. 5:18). For Maier, the central theme of the Bible's call to faith in the one, true God is evidence of the unity of the Testaments. The unity of the story told of the world and the creatures that God has made testifies to the unity of the Testaments. Jesus Christ, Maier writes, is "the turning point of the times," and "in him time has its 'fulfillment' and the 'fullness' of time makes its appearance."[56] Finally, Maier argues that the essential unity of Scripture is presupposed by the need of the church as the church formulates church doctrine and recognizes the theological character of its life. The interpretative approach to the two Testaments Maier advocates is that of "salvation-historical interpretation." Maier defines salvation history as "the activity of God, inseparably woven into history in its entirety, through which he effects his redeeming and perfecting will."[57] Only this method, he suggests, enables "observation of

The Relationship Between the Testaments

Subjective Theologies

Methodological Inclusivity	Methodological Exclusivity	Both/And Approaches	
Childs	Barr	Goldingay	Maier
seriously is to stress the special quality of the Old Testament's humanity which is reflected in the form of Israel's sacred scripture."[46] Childs, in his *Introduction,* says that while it lies beyond the scope of that present work to "establish the relation between the two testaments," "it is essential for a theological relationship to be maintained between the people of the Old Covenant and of the New. Regardless of whatever other writings or traditions were deemed authoritative by each community within a larger canon—for Jews it is the tradition of the sages—for Christians the gospel of Jesus Christ—the common canon of the Hebrew scriptures provides the fundamental basis for any serious relationship."[47]	theology is, before one begins to consider its adequacy and how one might appropriate it. From Barr, *The Concept,* 16.	New Testament rests on the foundation of the Old Testament.	the progressiveness and complexity of revelation."[58] The advantage of this approach is threefold, Maier writes: (1) "It does the most justice to the historical structure of revelation"; (2) "it embraces the fullness of revelation"; and (3) "it is best suited to express the unity of revelation in all its challenging complexity."[59]

42. Edgar V. McNight, *Postmodern Use of the Bible* (Nashville: Abingdon, 1988).
43. Ibid., 76.
44. Brevard Childs, *Introduction to the Old Testament as Scripture* (Philadelphia: Fortress, 1979), 73.
45. G. T. Sheppard, "Brevard Childs," in *Historical Handbook of Major Biblical Interpreters,* ed. Donald K. McKim (Downers Grove, IL: InterVarsity Press, 1999), 581.
46. Childs, *Introduction,* 71.
47. Ibid., 72.

50. Ibid., 186.
51. Ibid., 187.

52. John Goldingay, *Approaches to Old Testament Interpretation* (Downers Grove, IL: InterVarsity Press, 1981), 19.
53. Ibid.
54. Ibid., 34.
55. Ibid., 36.

56. Gerhard Maier, *Biblical Hermeneutics,* trans. Robert Yarbrough (Wheaton, IL: Crossway, 1994), 191–92.
57. Ibid., 196.
58. Ibid., 195.
59. Ibid.

Bibliography

Alexander, T. Desmond, and Brian S. Rosner, eds. *New Dictionary of Biblical Theology*. Downers Grove, IL: InterVarsity Press, 2000.

Altizer, Thomas J. J. "America and the Future of Theology." In *Radical Theology and the Death of God*. Edited by Thomas J. J. Altizer and William Hamilton. Indianapolis: Bobbs-Merrill, 1966.

———. *The Self-Embodiment of God*. New York: Harper and Row, 1977.

Augustine. *Confessions*. Translated by Henry Chadwick. Oxford: Oxford University Press, 1991.

———. *On Christian Doctrine*.

Baillie, John. *The Idea of Revelation in Recent Thought*. New York: Columbia University Press, 1954.

Baker, David L. *Two Testaments, One Bible: A Study of the Theological Relationship Between the Old and New Testaments*. 2d ed. Downers Grove, IL: InterVarsity Press, 1991.

Barr, James. "The Bible as Document of Believing Communities." In *The Bible As a Document of the University*. Edited by Hans Dieter Betz. Atlanta: Scholars Press, 1981.

———. *The Concept of Biblical Theology*. Minneapolis: Fortress, 1999.

Barth, Karl. *Church Dogmatics*. 2d ed. Edited by G. W. Bromiley and T. F. Torrance. Edinburgh: T & T Clark, 1975.

———. *God in Action*. Manhassett, NY: Round Table, 1963.

Bateman, Herbert W., IV, ed. *Three Central Issues in Contemporary Dispensationalism: A Comparison of Traditional and Progressive Views*. Grand Rapids: Kregel, 1999.

Berkhof, Louis. *Systematic Theology*. Reprint, Grand Rapids: Eerdmans, 1996.

Berkhouwer, G. C. "The Voice of Karl Barth." In *A Half Century of Theology*. Translated and edited by Lewis B. Smedes. Grand Rapids: Eerdmans, 1977.

Blaising, Craig A., and Darrel L. Bock. *Progressive Dispensationalism*. Wheaton, IL: Bridgepoint, 1993.

Bloesch, Donald. *Holy Scripture: Revelation, Inspiration, and Interpretation*. Downers Grove, IL: InterVarsity Press, 1994.

———. *A Theology of Word and Spirit: Authority and Method in Theology*. Downers Grove, IL: InterVarsity Press, 1992.

Bray, Gerald. *Biblical Interpretation: Past and Present*. Downers Grove, IL: InterVarsity Press, 1996.

Bromiley, Geoffrey. *Historical Theology: An Introduction*. Edinburgh: T & T Clark, 1994.

Brown, Colin, ed. *New International Dictionary of New Testament Theology*. Grand Rapids: Zondervan, 1971.

Brümmer, Vincent. *Speaking of a Personal God: An Essay in Philosophical Theology*. New York: Cambridge University Press, 1992.

Brunner, Emil. *Natural Theology: Comprising "Nature and Grace" by Professor Dr. Emil Brunner and the Reply "No!" by Dr. Karl Barth*. Translated by Peter Fraenkel. London: Centary, 1946.

———. "The Necessity for Dogmatics." In *The Christian Doctrine of God*. Translated by Olive Wyon. Philadelphia: Westminster, 1950.

———. *Truth as Encounter*. Philadelphia: Westminster, 1964.

Budick, Stanford, and Wolfgang Iser, eds. *Languages of the Unsayable: The Play of Negativity in Literature and Literary Theory*. New York: Columbia University Press, 1989.

Bultmann, Rudolf. *Existence and Faith*. London: Hodder & Stoughton, 1961.

———. "The Problem of Hermeneutics." In *Essays: Philosophical and Theological*. London: SCM, 1955.

Calvin, John. *Institutes of the Christian Religion*. 2 vols. Edited by John T. McNeill. Translated by Ford Lewis Battles. Philadelphia: Westminster, 1960.

Bibliography

———. "Subject Matter of the Present Work." In *Institutes of the Christian Religion*. From the French edition of 1560.

Cambridge Dictionary of Philosophy. Edited by Robert Audi. Cambridge, England: Cambridge University Press, 1999.

Caputo, John D., and Michael J. Scanlon, eds. *God, the Gift, and Postmodernism*. Bloomington, IN: Indiana University Press, 1999.

Carson, D. A. "The Role of Exegesis in Systematic Theology." In *Doing Theology in Today's World*. Edited by John D. Woodbridge and Thomas Edward McComiskey. Grand Rapids: Zondervan, 1991.

———. "Unity and Diversity in the New Testament: The Possibility of Systematic Theology." In *Scripture and Truth*. Edited by D. A. Carson and John Woodbridge. Grand Rapids: Baker, 1992.

Charry, Ellen T. *By the Renewing of Your Minds: The Pastoral Function of Christian Doctrine*. New York: Oxford University Press, 1997.

Childs, Brevard. *Introduction to the Old Testament As Scripture*. Philadelphia: Fortress, 1979.

Clark, David K. *To Know and Love God*. Wheaton, IL: Crossway, 2003.

Clark, Gordon. *A Christian View of Men and Things*. Grand Rapids: Eerdmans, 1952.

———. *Language and Theology*. Jefferson, MD: Trinity Foundation, 1980.

Clement of Alexandria. *Stromata* 1.28.3. In *The Christian Theology Reader,* by Alister McGrath. 2d ed. Oxford: Blackwell, 2001.

Cohen, Anthony P. *Self Consciousness: An Alternative Anthropology of Identity*. London: Routledge, 1994.

Cullman, Oscar. *Salvation in History*. London: SCM, 1967.

Cupitt, Don. "Post-Christianity." In *Religion, Modernity and Postmodernity*. Edited by Paul Heelas. Oxford: Blackwell, 1998.

———. Preface to—*Taking Leave of God*. New York: Crossroad, 1981.

Davies, Oliver, and Denys Turner, eds. *Silence and the Word: Negative Theology and Incarnation*. Cambridge: Cambridge University Press, 2002.

Davis, John Jefferson, ed. *The Necessity of Systematic Theology*. 2d ed. Grand Rapids: Baker, 1978.

De Chardin, P. Teilhard. *Christianity and Evolution*. Translated by RenÈ Hague. New York: Harcourt Brace Jovanovich, 1971.

Derrida, Jacques. "How to Avoid Speaking: Denials." In *Derrida and Negative Theology*. Edited by Harold Coward and Toby Foshay. New York: State University of New York Press, 1992.

Dulles, Avery. *Models of Revelation*. 2d ed. Maryknoll, NY: Orbis, 1994.

Feinberg, John S., ed. *Continuity and Discontinuity: Perspectives on the Relationship Between the Old and New Testaments*. Westchester, IL: Crossway, 1988.

Fowl, Stephen. *Engaging Scripture*. Oxford: Blackwell, 1998.

———. "The Ethics of Interpretation, or What's Left over After the Elimination of Meaning." In *The Bible in Three Dimensions: Essays in Celebration of Forty Years of Biblical Studies in the University of Sheffield*. Edited by David J. A. Clines, Stephen E. Fowl, and Stanley E. Porter. Journal for the Study of the Old Testament Supplement Series 87. Sheffield, England: Sheffield Academic Press, 1990.

Frame, John. *The Doctrine of the Knowledge of God*. Phillipsburg, NJ: Presbyterian & Reformed, 1987.

Goldingay, John. *Approaches to Old Testament Interpretation*. Downers Grove, IL: InterVarsity Press, 1981.

Goldsworthy, Graeme. "Relationship of Old Testament and New Testament." In *New Dictionary of Biblical Theology*. Downers Grove, IL: InterVarsity Press, 2000.

Grenz, Stanley J. *Renewing the Center: Evangelical Theology in a Post-Theological Era*. Grand Rapids: Baker, 2000.

———. *Revisioning Evangelical Theology*. Downers Grove, IL: InterVarsity Press, 1993.

Gutierrez, Gustavo. *A Theology of Liberation*. Edited and translated by C. Inda and J. Eagleson. Maryknoll, NY: Orbis, 1973.

Harrison, R. K. "Higher Criticism." In *Evangelical Dictionary of Theology*. Edited by Walter A. Elwell. Grand Rapids: Baker, 1984.

Hasel, Gerhard F. *Evangelical Dictionary of Theology*. Edited by Walter Elwell. Grand Rapids: Baker, 1984.

Henry, Carl F. H. *God, Revelation, and Authority*. 4 vols. Waco, TX: Word, 1976–82.

———. *God, Revelation, and Authority*. 2 vols. Reprint, Wheaton, IL: Crossway, 1999.

———. "The Priority of Divine Revelation: A Review Article." *Journal of the Evangelical Theological Society* (March 1984): 91.

Hirsch, E. D., Jr. *Validity in Interpretation*. New Haven, CT: Yale University Press, 1967.

Horton, Michael. "Who Needs Systematic Theology When We Have the Bible?" *Modern Reformation* (January–February 2003): 13–22.

James, William. *Pragmatism and Other Essays*. New York: Washington Square, 1963.

Joachim, Harold H. *The Nature of Truth*. Reprint, New York: Greenwood, 1969.

Johnson, Phillip. "Is There a Blind Watchmaker?" In *Reason in the Balance: The Case Against Naturalism in Science, Law and Education*. Downers Grove, IL: InterVarsity Press, 1995.

———. *The Right Questions: Truth, Meaning and Public Debate*. Downers Grove, IL: InterVarsity Press, 2002.

Jowett, Benjamin. *On the Interpretation of Scripture and Other Essays*. London: Routledge & Sons, 1907.

Kaufman, Gordon. *An Essay on Theological Method*. Atlanta: Scholars Press, 1995.

Kermode, Frank. *The Classic: Literary Images of Permanence and Change*. Cambridge, MA: Harvard University Press, 1975.

Kerr, Hugh Thomson. *A Compend of Luther's Theology*. Philadelphia: Westminster, 1966.

Kirkham, Richard L. "Truth, correspondence theory of." In *Routledge Encyclopedia of Philosophy*. Edited by Edward Craig. New York: Routledge, n.d.

Lindbeck, George. *The Nature of Doctrine: Religion and Theology in a Postliberal Age*. Philadelphia: Westminster, 1984.

Lints, Richard. *The Fabric of Theology*. Grand Rapids: Eerdmans, 1993.

———. "Thinking Systematically About Theology." *Modern Reformation* (January–February 2003): 23.

Luther, Martin. "The Magnificat." *Works of Martin Luther*. 6 vols. Philadelphia: Muhlenberg, 1915–43.

———. *Prefaces to the Old Testament: Martin Luther's Basic Theological Writings*. Edited by Timothy F. Lull. Minneapolis: Fortress, 1989.

———. "A Treatise on Christian Liberty." In *Martin Luther's Basic Theological Writings*. Edited by Timothy F. Lull. Minneapolis: Fortress, 1989.

Maier, Gerhard. *Biblical Hermeneutics*. Translated by Robert Yarbrough. Wheaton, IL: Crossway, 1994.

Mascall, E. L. *The Openness of Being: Natural Theology Today*. Philadelphia: Westminster, 1971.

McClendon, James William. *Ethics: Systematic Theology*. Rev. ed. Nashville: Abingdon, 2002.

McDowell, Josh. *Evidence That Demands a Verdict: Historical Evidences for the Christian Faith*. San Bernardino, CA: Campus Crusade for Christ, 1972.

McGrath, Alister. *The Christian Theology Reader*. 2d ed. Oxford: Blackwell, 2001.

———. *The Genesis of Doctrine: A Study in the Foundation of Doctrinal Criticism*. Oxford: Blackwell, 1990.

———. *A Scientific Theology*. Grand Rapids: Eerdmans, 2001.

McKnight, Edgar V. *Postmodern Use of the Bible*. Nashville: Abingdon, 1988.

Migliore, Daniel. *Faith Seeking Understanding*. Grand Rapids: Eerdmans, 1991.

Moreland, J. P., and William Lane Craig. *Philosophical Foundations for a Christian Worldview*. Downers Grove, IL: InterVarsity Press, 2003.

Moser, Paul K., Dwayne H. Mulder, and J. D. Trout. *The Theory of Knowledge: A Thematic Introduction*. New York: Oxford University Press, 1998.

Muller, Richard. "The Role of Church History in the Study of Systematic Theology." In *Doing Theology in*

Today's World. Edited by John D. Woodbridge and Thomas Edward McComiskey. Grand Rapids: Zondervan, 1991.

The New Scofield Reference Bible. New York: Oxford University Press, 1967.

Niebuhr, H. Richard. *The Meaning of Revelation*. New York: Macmillan, 1941.

O'Brien, Thomas C. "Truth." In *Encyclopedic Dictionary of Religion*. Edited by Paul Kevin Meagher, Thomas C. O'Brien, and Consuelo Maria Aherne. Washington, DC: Corpus, 1979.

Olliphant, Scott. "The Consistency of Van Til's Methodology." *Westminster Theological Journal* 52.1 (Spring 1990): 35.

Packer, J. I. "Is Systematic Theology a Mirage? An Introductory Discussion." In *Doing Theology in Today's World*. Edited by John D. Woodbridge and Thomas Edward McComiskey. Grand Rapids: Zondervan, 1991.

Padgett, Alan G. "Immanuel Kant." In *The Dictionary of Historical Theology*. Edited by Trevor Hart. Grand Rapids: Eerdmans, 2000.

Pascal, Blaise. *Pensees*. Paris: Editions du Seuil, 1962.

Philips, T. R., and D. L. Okholm, eds. *The Nature of Confession: Evangelicals and Postliberals in Conversation*. Downers Grove, IL: InterVarsity Press, 1996.

Reventlow, Henning Graf. *Problems of Biblical Theology in the Twentieth Century*. Philadelphia: Fortress, 1986.

Rubenstein, Richard L., and John K. Roth, eds. *The Politics of Latin American Liberation Theology*. Washington, DC: Institute Press, 1988.

Ruether, Rosemary Radford. "Foundations for a Theology of Liberation." In *Liberation Theology*. New York: Paulist, 1972.

———. "The Task of Feminist Theology." In *Doing Theology in Today's World*. Edited by John D. Woodbridge and Thomas Edward McComiskey. Grand Rapids: Zondervan, 1991.

Runzo, Joseph, and Craig Ihara, eds. *Religious Experience and Religious Belief: Essays in the Epistemology of Religion*. Lanham, MD: University Press of America, 1986.

Ryrie, Charles. "Dispensationalism." In *Evangelical Dictionary of Theology*. Edited by Walter A. Elwell. Grand Rapids: Baker, 1984.

Schleiermacher, Friedrich D. E. *The Christian Faith*. Edited by H. R. Mackintosh and J. S. Stewart. Reprint, New York: Harper & Row, 1963.

———. *The Christian Faith*. 2d ed. Edited by H. R. Mackintosh and J. S. Stewart. Edinburgh: T & T Clark, 1989.

Sheppard, G. T. "Brevard Childs." In *Historical Handbook of Major Biblical Interpreters*. Edited by Donald K. McKim. Downers Grove, IL: InterVarsity Press, 1999.

Stiver, Dan. *The Philosophy of Religious Language*. Oxford: Blackwell, 1994.

Stout, Jeffrey. "What Is the Meaning of a Text?" *New Literary History* 14 (1982): 1–12.

Taylor, Mark C. *Deconstructing Theology*. New York: Crossroad, 1982.

Tertullian. "On the Flesh of Christ." In *Ante-Nicene Fathers*. Edited by Alexander Roberts and James Donaldson. 2d ed. Vol. 3. Reprint, Peabody, MA: Hendrickson, 1999.

Thiel, John E. *Nonfoundationalism*. Minneapolis: Fortress, 1991.

Thielicke, Helmut. *The Evangelical Faith*. 2 vols. Translated and edited by G. W. Bromiley. Grand Rapids: Eerdmans, 1974.

Thiselton, Anthony C. *The Two Horizons: New Testament Hermeneutics and Philosophical Description with Special Reference to Heidegger, Bultmann, Gadamer, and Wittgenstein*. Grand Rapids: Eerdmans, 1980.

Thomas Aquinas. *Summa Theologiae*. In *The Christian Theology Reader*, by Alister McGrath. Oxford: Blackwell, 1995.

———. *The Summa Theologica*. In *Introduction to Thomas Aquinas*. Edited by Anton C. Pegis. New York: Modern Library, 1948.

Thomas, Robert L. *Evangelical Hermeneutics*. Grand Rapids: Kregel, 2002.

Tilley, Terrance. *Talking of God: An Introduction to Philosophical Analysis of Religious Language*. New York: Paulist, 1978.

Torrance, Thomas F. *Reality and Scientific Theology*. Edinburgh: Scottish Academic Press, 1985.

———. *Theological Science*. London: Oxford University Press, 1969.

———. *Theology in Reconstruction*. Grand Rapids: Eerdmans, 1965.

Tracy, David. *The Analogical Imagination: Christian Theology and the Culture of Pluralism*. New York: Crossroad, 2000.

Troeltsch, Ernst. "Faith and History." In *Religion in History*. Translated by James Luther Adams and Walter F. Bense. Edinburgh: T & T Clark, 1991.

Turner, J. David. *An Introduction to Liberation Theology*. New York: University Press of America, 1994.

Vanhoozer, Kevin J. *The Drama of Doctrine: A Canonical-linguistic Approach to Christian Theology*. Louisville: Westminster/John Knox, 2005.

———. "God's Mighty Speech Acts." In *First Theology*. Downers Grove, IL: InterVarsity Press, 2002.

———. *Is There a Meaning in This Text? The Bible, the Reader, and the Reality of Literary Knowledge*. Grand Rapids: Zondervan, 1998.

Van Huyssteen, J. Wentzel. *Essays in Postfoundationalist Theology*. Grand Rapids: Eerdmans, 1997.

Van Til, Cornelius. *Apologetics*. Philadelphia: Westminster Theological Seminary, 1971.

———. *A Christian Theory of Knowledge*. Philadelphia: Presbyterian & Reformed, 1969.

Von Harnack, Adolph. *What Is Christianity?* Translated by Thomas Bailey Saunders. Reprint, New York: Harper & Brothers, 1957.

Vos, Geerhardus. *Biblical Theology: Old and New Testaments*. Grand Rapids: Eerdmans, 1954.

Warfield, B. B. "The Idea of Systematic Theology." In *Studies in Theology*. Vol. 9 of *The Works of Benjamin B. Warfield*. Reprint, Grand Rapids: Baker, 1981.

Watson, Francis. *Text and Truth: Redefining Biblical Theology*. Grand Rapids: Eerdmans, 1997.

———. *Text, Church and World: Biblical Interpretation in Theological Perspective*. Grand Rapids: Eerdmans, 1994.

Webb, William. *Slaves, Women and Homosexuals: Exploring the Hermeneutics of Cultural Analysis*. Downers Grove, IL: InterVarsity Press, 2001.

White, James Emery. *What Is Truth?* Nashville: Broadman & Holman, 1994.

Wolterstorff, Nicholas. *Divine Discourse: Philosophical Reflections on the Claim That God Speaks*. Cambridge, MA: Cambridge University Press, 1995.

Wright, G. Ernest. *God Who Acts*. London: SCM, 1966.

Scripture Index

Name Index

Charts *on* Prolegomena

Subject Index

Subject Index

Subject Index